"In the studies that I have examined on the impact of [Maharishi's Yogic Flying program] on conflict, I can find no methodological flaws, and the findings have been consistent across a large number of replications in many different geographical and conflictual situations. As unlikely as the premise may sound, I think we have to take these studies seriously."

Ted Robert Gurr, Ph.D., author, **Violence in America,** *Bantam* **Books** *and U.S. Government Printing Office, Distinguished University Professor, Department of Government and Politics, University of Maryland*

"This book describes an unprecedented breakthrough in our ability to understand and seriously address the fundamental problems of violence and terrorism."

Dr. John Davies, Ph.D., Co-Director, Partners in Conflict and Partners in Peacebuilding Projects, Center for International Development and Conflict Management, University of Maryland

"The claim can be plausibly made that the potential impact of this research exceeds that of any other ongoing social or psychological research program. The research has survived a broader array of statistical tests than most research in the field of conflict resolution. I think this work, and the theory that informs it, deserve the most serious consideration by academics and policy makers alike."

David Edwards, Ph.D.
Professor of Government at the University of Texas at Austin

"The data show an impressive, statistically significant correlation: a decrease in violent crime for the time period over which the group meditated."

Beverly Rubik, Ph.D., Biophysicist and President of the Institute for Frontier Science in Oakland, California

"The possibility is that we have made one of the most important discoveries of our time."

Dr. Juan Pascual-Leone,
Professor Emeritus, York University in Ottawa, Canada, a member of the review board of the **Journal of Conflict Resolution**

"I want to express my support for this research. What we really are looking at here I think is a new paradigm of viewing crime and violence...."

Anne Hughes
Ph.D., Professor of Sociology, University of District of Columbia

"I was initially skeptical, but having studied the research completed to date, I have concluded that these studies on the [Vedic peace technologies] have subjected theory to proper empirical tests. They have shown sound results which demand serious interest. This method should be applied more widely in programs to reduce crime."

Ken Pease, Ph.D., Professor of Criminology, University of Huddersfield. Board Member, British Home Office National Crime Prevention Board, 1993–96, Chairman of CIRAC, Centre for the Independent Research and Analysis of Crime

"I have been following the research on Maharishi's [defense] as it has developed over the last twenty years. There is now a strong and coherent body of evidence showing that [this approach] provides a simple and cost-effective solution to many of the social problems we face today. This research and its conclusions are so strong, that it demands action from those responsible for government policy."

Huw Dixon, Ph.D., Professor of Economics,
York University, England

"People have to know there is no political or educational solution to the problems in Iraq, Iran, Israel, and Palestine. It is impossible to educate everyone, using conventional means of education. There is too much propaganda, too much government influence over the educational system, and too many poor people to try to educate. However, Maharishi's program wakes the people up and melts their hard feelings, producing the effect that is the goal of a good educational system."

Payman Salek, a Muslim engineer from Iran, who learned the Transcendental Meditation technique in Iran in 1988 and became a Yogic Flyer in 1993

VICTORY BEFORE WAR

VICTORY BEFORE WAR

Preventing Terrorism through the
Vedic Peace Technologies of
His Holiness Maharishi Mahesh Yogi

by **Robert Keith Wallace, Ph.D., and Jay B. Marcus**

Foreword by John Hagelin, Ph.D.
Afterword by Dr. Bevan Morris

MAHARISHI UNIVERSITY OF MANAGEMENT PRESS
FAIRFIELD, IOWA

Maharishi University of Management Press

Fairfield, Iowa 52557 USA

Published in 2005

Printed in the United States of America

8 7 6 5 4 3 2 1

Library of Congress Cataloging-in-Publication Data

is available on request.

ISBN 0-923569-38-3

Library of Congress Catalog Card Number: 2005006124

TABLE OF CONTENTS

SPECIAL ACKNOWLEDGMENT

The Vedic peace technologies are based on a vast body of knowledge, the Vedic literature, a timeless wisdom that has been maintained by the enlightened masters of the ancient Vedic tradition of India. The application of this knowledge in the field of defense was first set forth in 1996 by His Holiness Maharishi Mahesh Yogi in his book, *Maharishi's Absolute Theory of Defense* (available from Maharishi University of Management Press). Maharishi's book, other writings by Maharishi, and Maharishi's lectures and recent press conferences form the basis for the material in this book.

FOREWORD

How can we create a lasting state of world peace in this age of nuclear overkill and weapons of mass destruction? Scientific advances now allow small countries or even small groups of individuals to threaten the security of entire nations. Biological and chemical weapons are widely available and can be easily transported across national borders. Conventional military strategies for homeland defense have become increasingly irrelevant, and no one is truly secure.

We urgently need a new, more fundamental approach to peace that can neutralize the very basis of terrorism and war. *Victory Before War* by Dr. Robert Keith Wallace and Jay Marcus presents just such an approach. Maharishi's proven, practical technology for preventing terrorism has been validated by almost 50 studies published in leading peer-reviewed scientific journals. This approach is a technological application of the most advanced discoveries in the fields of quantum mechanics, neuroscience, and human consciousness.

From June through July 1993, I directed a two-month scientific research experiment using this peace-creating technology in Washington, D.C. The study, which brought approximately 4,000 project participants to the District, resulted in a marked reduction in the level of violent crime. The statistical probability that this outcome could have reflected chance variation in crime levels was less than 2 in a billion (p < .000000002) (*Social Indicators Research* 47: 153-201, 1999). A remarkable calm descended upon the city: a tense atmosphere of police sirens, audible gunshots, and rancorous partisan bickering and Congressional gridlock was suddenly transformed into palpable peace, social harmony, and a new spirit of bipartisan cooperation.

But this study is only one of 50. This peace-based approach, described fully in this book, has been subjected to extensive scientific investigation during the past 25 years and repeatedly shown to defuse acute ethnic, political, and religious tensions; to quell violence and open warfare in war-torn areas; and to dramatically reduce global terrorism. Many of these applications took the form of carefully controlled experiments, and the findings withstood rigorous, anonymous peer review and were published in leading scientific journals. In study after study, this approach has successfully reduced crime, violence, and terrorism in tests conducted at local, statewide, national, and international levels. It has worked every time, and now has the support of hundreds of scientists who have examined the technology and its associated research.

This new approach to homeland defense calls for the immediate establishment of large, permanent groups of peace-creating experts practicing specific "technologies of consciousness" that have been scientifically shown to neutralize the societal tensions that fuel violence, terrorism, and social conflict. Such groups create a measurable effect of harmony and peace throughout society.

While conventional technologies are based on the application of specific, isolated laws of nature functioning at the chemical, biological, and nuclear levels, this new approach is based on the discovery of a completely holistic level of natural law that is vastly more fundamental and powerful than even the nuclear force. Consequently, this technology

- Can easily overpower—and effectively disarm—conventional technologies of offense based on the chemical, biological, or nuclear levels;
- Creates pervasive and inescapable results, since it works from the most comprehensive and holistic level of natural law; and
- Is inherently safe, despite its power, with effects that are broadly life-supporting and free from unanticipated negative side effects.

Now all of us—citizens and governmental leaders alike—must act immediately to implement this approach widely and thereby uphold national security and global peace. We would be irresponsible to do otherwise.

In *Victory Before War*, the authors have created a powerful and compelling manual for creating permanent world peace. I urge all well-wishers of peace to read it carefully and then take every possible action to bring its vision to fruition, for the sake of our generation and all generations to come.

—*John Hagelin, Ph.D.*
Dr. Hagelin is one of the world's foremost physicists and a winner of the prestigious Kilby Award. He is the president of the U.S. Peace Government and director of the Institute of Science, Technology and Public Policy at Maharishi University of Management in Fairfield, Iowa.

ONE

An Introduction to Maharishi's Vedic Defense

"The hypothesis [that violence can be prevented by Maharishi's Yogic Flying program] definitely raised some eyebrows among our reviewers. But the statistical work is sound. The numbers are there. When you can statistically control for as many variables as these studies do, it makes the results much more convincing. This evidence indicates that we now have a new technology to generate peace in the world."

Raymond Russ, Ph.D.
Professor of Psychology, University of Maine
Editor, Journal of Mind and Behavior

The Source of Maharishi's Homeland Defense

The Vedic peace technologies constitute the world's most ancient and complete homeland defense. In this age, these technologies have been revived by His Holiness Maharishi Mahesh Yogi, who has devoted his life to applying the Vedic wisdom to solve the problems of modern times. These peace technologies, including the Transcendental Meditation® and Yogic Flying programs and what are known as *Yagya* performances, are derived from the Vedic literature of India, the oldest records of human knowledge and human development, which have been maintained by the great sages of the Vedic tradition.

The Vedic Tradition

To those with some familiarity with the Vedic knowledge, the Vedic tradition is itself an important validation of Maharishi's peace technologies.

Maharishi Mahesh Yogi

In the East, a sage's tradition is of great importance, much more so than in the West, where we may speak of the college or university that someone attended, or, for lawyers, the judge for whom someone clerked. In the community of yogis and enlightened sages in India, a man is known by his particular tradition of knowledge, and in this community, Vedic knowledge is recognized as the supreme knowledge of life. Maharishi's Vedic tradition is the world's most ancient tradition, which means that the knowledge of this tradition has credibility—it has stood the test of time. This tradition is represented by an unbroken line of India's most respected masters of the techniques for human development, including Shankara, Vyasa, and Vashishta, names that are well known by Indian scholars. These great sages discovered the means to fully develop human consciousness for the benefit of the individual and the society.

In this age, the current revival of Vedic wisdom began with Maharishi's teacher, His Divinity Brahmananda Saraswati, regarded as one of India's greatest teachers in the Vedic tradition. Maharishi absorbed the complete experience and understanding of Vedic wisdom under his teacher's guidance, and then began its formal restoration.

Maharishi's Principal Focus the Past 25 Years

Maharishi introduced the Transcendental Meditation (TM®) program to the West in the 1960s and 1970s, traveling first to the United States and to parts of Europe. Now over five million individuals have learned the TM technique. The program's popularity results from the many benefits people experience, as evidenced by a considerable body of research on the ability of this program to relieve stress disorders, including high blood pressure. The National Institutes of Health have awarded over $18 million to study the clinical application of the Transcendental Meditation program, particularly for the reduction of hypertension and heart disease. Today physicians recommend the program to their patients, and executives bring it into the boardroom.

While the TM program is now considered mainstream, lowering stress and reducing high blood pressure have not been his principal focus in the last 25 years. Due to wars and the growing worldwide threat of terrorism, Maharishi's principal focus has been the development of the ancient Vedic peace technologies to prevent acts of mass destruction. These strategies are traditionally understood to provide a *complete* defense against terrorist acts. Maharishi has explained that what is incomplete about all of today's systems of defense is the approach of trying to destroy the enemy, when the enemy is unseen.

A Good Offense Is the Best Defense May Apply to Football, but Does It Apply to Terrorism?

In his address to the National Defense University in February 2002, Donald Rumsfeld, Secretary of Defense, stated:

> It is not possible to defend against every conceivable kind of attack in every conceivable location at every minute of the day or night. Defending against terrorism and other emerging 21st century threats may well require that we take the war to the enemy. The best, and in some cases, the only defense, is a good offense.

In 2002, at the time of the passage of the law creating a Homeland Security Department, Tom Ridge, the former head of U.S. homeland security, made the same point—that the best defense is a good offense, and this is certainly President Bush's philosophy. Everyone acknowledges, however, that there will be more successful attacks on U.S. soil (the 9/11 Commission Report says, "we are not safe"). This is because terrorists and motivated criminals are largely unseen, and have the advantage of waiting for their opportunities. Sooner or later there will be cracks in our security.

The prevailing wisdom in the fight against terrorism derives from the football axiom that the best defense is a good offense. Due to the difficulty of defending ourselves, Washington is compelled to favor an aggressive military offense, which allows the president to choose his targets. However, unlike football where you are either on offense or defense, and the more you are on offense, the less important the defense, with terrorism, the opposite is true. With terrorism, the more we take the offensive, the more we invite retaliation. Therefore, it is crucial to be able to defend ourselves from those with access to both crude weapons and modern technologies of space, chemical, biological, and genetic warfare.

Preemptive and "preventive" wars also carry risks not typically considered in the Western world. Maharishi explains that according to the Vedic perspective, there are inevitable, harmful consequences from killing other human beings. The Vedic tradition is the origin of the concept of *karma*, which states that for every action there is an opposite and equal reaction. We see this same principle echoed in many great traditions in expressions like "As you sow, so shall you reap," or "measure for measure" (from Judaism's Talmud), meaning that if you rob or kill, you will be robbed or killed in return. For most people, however, such expressions are simply based on theory or hypothesis, and "As you sow, so shall you reap" is not held to be an immutable law of nature, which is the Vedic perspective. In Chapter 2, in excerpts from an interview on the Larry King television show in May 2002, Maharishi explains the principle of karma in the context of the September 11 attacks, and he warns America that those who kill will themselves be destroyed.

> Maharishi explains the principle of karma in the context of the September 11 attacks, and he warns America that those who kill will themselves be destroyed.

The Principles Involved in a Complete Defense against Terrorism

If true defensive strategies are crucial to each nation's safety, what then could be the nature of a complete defense against terrorism taking into account that terrorists, for the most part, cannot be discovered before they inflict damage?

An act of terrorism begins in the human mind, and it is there that it must be stopped. If, however, we can't readily locate the terrorist in an effort to change his thinking, the only effective approach will be to neutralize intense negativity in the thinking of everyone in a particular area, including the extreme negativity of the would-be terrorist. How is this possible? Western approaches to changing a person's thinking through conventional education or persuasion, or through punishment or fear-based approaches, will not change terrorist thinking. Terrorists are martyrs. They believe that God is on their side, and no amount of persuasion, intellectual debate, or saber rattling will change their desire to strike a blow for their cause.

Maharishi's Vedic defense, on the other hand, does not depend on these conventional approaches. This defense uses highly specific Vedic procedures that prevent violent thoughts, and therefore violent acts, from arising in the consciousness of everyone in the vicinity of those participating in Maharishi's defense program *without the necessity of any direct intellectual or physical contact with the terrorist.*

Unfortunately, in today's society, doubts and disinterest begin to surface once reference is made to "consciousness" and especially a program intended to change the level of consciousness of others without any direct contact with the terrorist. Most people have difficulty defining consciousness or pinpointing how they can change their own consciousness, let alone change the consciousness of a terrorist at a distance who is completely uninterested in change. The knowledge of consciousness, however, is the principal domain of Maharishi's Vedic tradition.

Maharishi explains that consciousness literally means the state of being conscious or aware. Consciousness, being primary to all experience, underlies all our thinking, feeling, and activity. Consciousness is what must be present to allow us to feel happy or angry or be violent or show compassion.

Maharishi also explains that consciousness, like an ocean, has an active surface level and a silent level, sometimes described as the "deepest" or most settled state of consciousness. From the quiet depth of consciousness thoughts emerge, become more developed, and are acted upon or rejected when they surface in our awareness.

Physical Activity
Thinking and Feeling
Consciousness

In the diagram below, a thought, represented by a bubble, begins at the depth of consciousness and rises in the mind, represented by an ocean. By the time the thought rises to the surface (point A in the illustration), it has developed enough to be appreciated as a thought by what may be considered the conscious mind.

During the practice of the Transcendental Meditation technique, the meditator begins at the active surface level of the mind (point A) and, using the technique he has been taught, effortlessly allows the mind to experience increasingly subtler stages of thinking, until the mind experiences the quiet depth of human consciousness—pure consciousness—from where thoughts begin to emerge. The meditator "transcends" (goes beyond) even the experience of the subtlest state of thought and experiences what Maharishi describes as the "transcendental field," an underlying field connecting everyone and everything.

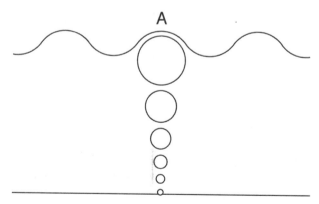

Transcendental Field

Here is the key to Maharishi's Vedic defense: If the terrorist's consciousness can be influenced at this fundamental level—from where all thoughts and feelings emerge—his thinking and behavior will automatically change in a way that no amount of debate or persuasion could ever accomplish. Of course, the terrorist does not make himself available to us in our effort to change his state of mind. But, fortunately, the terrorist's lack of availability and lack of interest in any change is irrelevant to Maharishi's Vedic peace technologies because of one other crucial understanding about the nature of consciousness.

Everyone and Everything Is Connected through the Transcendental Field

The Vedic knowledge holds that it is possible to influence everyone through the Vedic peace technologies because everyone is connected through the transcendental field. Maharishi explains that when an individual practicing the Transcendental Meditation technique experiences the transcendental field, he enlivens the field, automatically radiating an influence to everyone in the vicinity through what physicists call the *field effect*. This effect can be seen in the laws of nature governing the functioning of the atoms in the laser device, as well as the laws of nature affecting human consciousness and the human physiology. In the laser, the individual atoms generate light, enlivening the electromagnetic field. As long as the enlivenment of the electromagnetic field is weak, the individual atoms function in a disorderly manner, moving randomly and banging into one another. However, once the enlivenment of the field exceeds a critical threshold, the field effect gives rise to a phase transition and all atoms begin to function coherently, producing laser light with its extraordinary properties.

Phase Transition towards Coherence Due to Field Effect

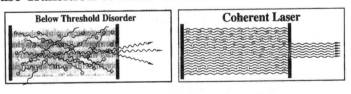

Phase Transition from ➡ Disorder to Coherence

Similarly, when a large group experiences the transcendental field at the same time through the group practice of the Vedic peace technologies, they have a correspondingly great effect in enlivening the transcendental field. Once the field is enlivened by a critical threshold (number) of experts in the Vedic peace technologies, just as all the atoms in the laser device begin to function coherently, the field effect results in all individuals in the vicinity of the Vedic experts experiencing an influence of coherence and peace, defusing religious and cultural stress and inhibiting violent tendencies.

To explain the phenomenon of influencing others from the level of the transcendental field, Maharishi sometimes uses the analogy of dropping a pebble into a pond. The pebble creates a faint ripple in the pond, which is experienced by those close enough to where the pebble has dropped. However, when many individuals perform the Vedic peace technologies together, at the same time, from the same location, the ripple in the transcendental field becomes a powerful wave resulting in a measurable, peaceful influence on those in the vicinity.

The Interconnectedness at Fundamental Levels

Modern science has actually come to the same conclusions concerning the interconnectedness of everything at fundamental levels, as explained more fully in Chapter 4. While matter appears as separate on some levels of nature, quantum physics describes everything as fundamentally interconnected through underlying, continuous fields which pervade the universe. Modern physics has discovered a unified field of natural law underlying the four fundamental forces of nature (see the chart below), giving rise to all natural phenomena.

According to Maharishi, the unified field discovered by modern science is the transcendental field. Maharishi explains that the unified field or transcendental field is experienced during the Transcendental Meditation technique as "pure consciousness." Whatever we may call this field, what is important is that everyone is connected through it, making it possible for the meditator group to influence everyone in their vicinity when they experience pure consciousness.

The Interconnectedness of Everything
Through the Transcendental Field

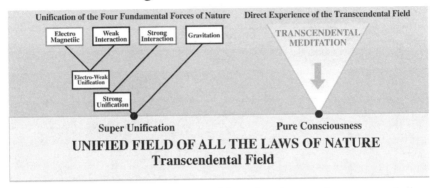

Everyone knows that a central broadcasting station can send electronic waves through the electromagnetic field, permitting everyone with a television to receive the signals.

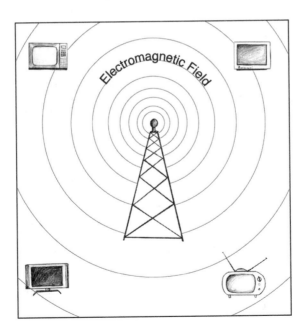

Similarly, Maharishi's experts in the Vedic peace technologies are like the central broadcasting station. In this analogy, the human brain (which can be thought of as the home of consciousness in the body) is the transmitter and receiver, and everyone within range of those "broadcasting" the influence is instantaneously affected.

The approach of Maharishi's Vedic defense is summarized by the ancient Sanskrit phrase, *Tat sannidau vaira tyagah:* "In the vicinity of Yoga, hostile tendencies are eliminated." Yoga, here, refers not to stretching exercises, but to the perfectly peaceful and coherent state of consciousness that is the ultimate goal of Yoga. Maharishi's programs utilize advanced Vedic procedures, known today as the Transcendental Meditation and TM-Sidhi® programs, including the Yogic Flying technique. Maharishi's programs involve groups of individuals, who participate in these Vedic peace technologies at the same time of day. The group practice has been found to be crucial. A measurable peaceful and coherent influence is radiated to everyone in the vicinity when a sufficient number of people practice the Vedic peace technologies together.

To the observer, the initial stage of the Yogic Flying practice results in the body lifting or hopping off the ground in a series of short hops. Though not apparent to the observer, this lifting of the body is based solely on a simple mental performance (rather than a gymnastic effort). However, as Maharishi emphasizes, the technique is not only valued for its outer effect, but also for its ability to create a maximum peaceful and coherent effect in the consciousness of those practicing the technique and a corresponding effect in the vicinity of the practitioners. The research on the Yogic Flying program is contained in Chapter 5 and summarized below.[1]

Three Yogic Flyers. The foam mattress is to cushion their landing.

Yogic Flyers in Europe

Yogic Flying demonstration in Des Moines, Iowa

Timing a Yogic Flyer during his performance

Measuring brain coherence during Yogic Flying

Peace Research

Over 30 years ago, research on the first of Maharishi's peace technologies to be introduced to the Western world—the Transcendental Meditation technique—showed that the practice of the technique produces not only a subjectively peaceful and settled state, but a unique orderliness or coherence in the functioning of the brain. Modern science has discovered that for every mental state there is a corresponding physical state and that the functioning of consciousness is directly related to the functioning of the brain and nervous system. The waking, sleeping, and dreaming states of consciousness, for example, have their unique brain functioning, which can be measured and identified by looking at the activity of the brain. Similarly, during the practice of the Transcendental Meditation technique, we can verify that a profound change in consciousness is occurring by looking at the unique brain activity during the technique. The charts below use a computer-generated picture to show the increasing brain wave coherence as an individual continues his practice of the Transcendental Meditation technique over a period of time.

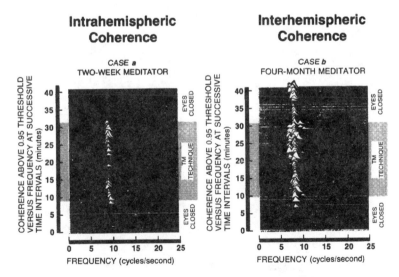

The peaks in the chart are computer drawn and indicate especially strong coherence at different brain wave frequencies. The charts show the level of coherence during three periods: (1) when the individual is sitting with his eyes closed at the beginning of the TM technique; (2) during the actual 20-minute practice of the TM technique; and (3) after meditation when the eyes are still closed. As can be seen in the case of the two-week meditator, a relatively strong coherence is apparent only during the practice of the TM technique. However, as the individual continues to practice the TM technique, coherence is generated throughout the entire brain and is evident before, during, and after meditation. Importantly, Maharishi's Yogic Flying program has been found to produce the maximum brain coherence, and, therefore, it has maximum utility in Maharishi's Vedic defense program. As will be explained in Chapter 4, the coherence in consciousness is correlated with more settled and peaceful states of consciousness. The least excited state of mind is the most coherent state of mind.

Optimizing Brain Functioning

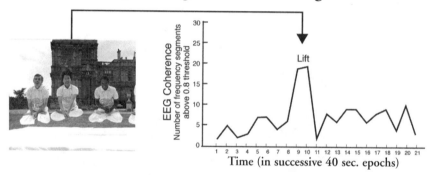

Maximum brain coherence during Yogic Flying occurs just before lift off.

Maharishi's program to generate peace and coherence in the collective consciousness is a new paradigm in our understanding of how thought and action can be changed, but it is not mere theory or speculation. For many who have looked deeply into this program, initial skepticism has been replaced by enthusiasm (see the endorsements at the beginning of the book). Research has documented reductions in hostilities during Maharishi's Vedic defense campaigns conducted in Rhodesia, the

Philippines, Central America, the U.S., England, Holland, New Delhi, Puerto Rico, Australia, and elsewhere. To date, approximately 50 small-scale studies show significant reductions in violence when a sufficient number of experts utilize the Vedic peace technologies.

Decreased Crime Rate in U.S. Cities

Change in crime rate 1972-1973: Cities with one percent of the population practicing the TM technique compared to control cities

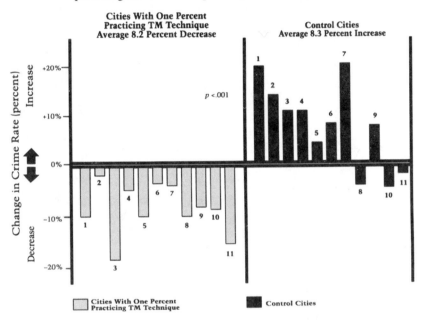

City Name	Percent Change	City Name	Percent Change
1. Chapel Hill, NC	-9.3%	1. Rocky Mount, NC	+20.2%
2. Ithaca, NY	-0.6%	2. Poughkeepsie, NY	+14.4%
3. Lawrence, KS	-18.4%	3. Lafayette, IN	+11.1%
4. Bloomington, IN	-4.5%	4. Columbia, MO	+11.2%
5. Carbondale, IL	-9.9%	5. Marshalltown, IA	+5.0%
6. Iowa City, IA	-2.5%	6. Oshkosh, WI	+8.3%
7. Ames, IA	-3.6%	7. Norman, OK	+20.8%
8. Boulder, CO	-9.1%	8. Fort Collins, CO	-3.2%
9. Santa Cruz, CA	-7.9%	9. Monterey, CA	+8.5%
10. Santa Barbara, CA	-8.8%	10. Costa Mesa, CA	-3.9%
11. Los Altos, CA	-16.4%	11. Claremont, CA	-1.4%

Improved International Relations

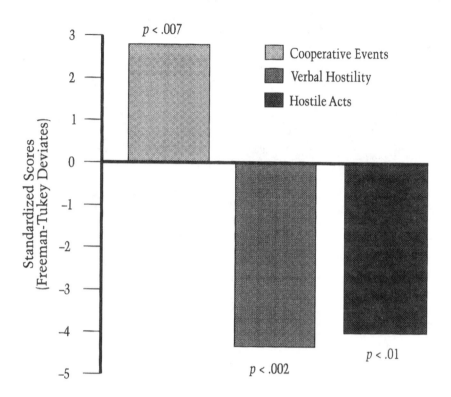

During a 10-week period in 1978, when peace-creating groups of participants in Maharishi's Transcendental Meditation and Yogic Flying program went to five major trouble-spot areas in the world, international relations improved—verbal hostility and hostile acts declined, and cooperative events increased. The improvements in these three conflict-scale categories were determined by time series analysis of worldwide data from the Conflict and Peace Data Bank International File.

Reference: Orme-Johnson, Dillbeck, Bousquet, & Alexander, 1985.

Increased Positivity of Events in
Situations of International Conflict

Percent of Total Events as Rated for Degree of Conflict

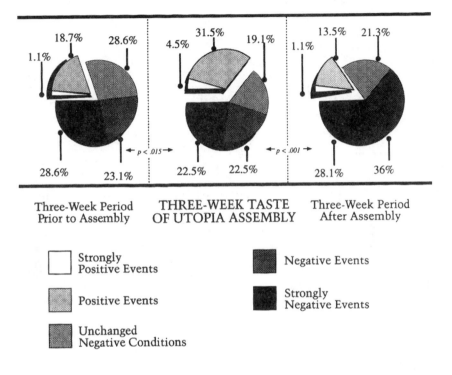

Three-Week Period Prior to Assembly	THREE-WEEK TASTE OF UTOPIA ASSEMBLY	Three-Week Period After Assembly

◻ Strongly Positive Events

■ Negative Events

▨ Positive Events

■ Strongly Negative Events

▨ Unchanged Negative Conditions

SOURCE: Content Analysis of *The New York Times*

During the three-week period of the Taste of Utopia Assembly in Iowa involving 7,000 Yogic Flyers (December 1983 to January 1984), the balance of negativity to positivity in events pertaining to international conflicts in the trouble-spot areas of the world shifted significantly towards increased positivity. After the Assembly the balance of events reverted towards increased negativity.

Reference: Orme-Johnson, Cavanaugh, Alexander, Gelderloos, Dillbeck, Lanford, & Abou Nader, 1987.

In one of the initial studies in 1977 (see chart on page 15), researchers found that in 11 cities where just 1% of the population had been instructed in the Transcendental Meditation technique, there was an average 16.5% decrease in the crime rate as compared to 11 control cities having the same characteristics, but without significant TM meditators.[2] Then in 1978, it was found that similar results could be achieved with even a smaller percentage of individuals participating in Maharishi's advanced Yogic Flying program. Maharishi, therefore, began sending groups of his Yogic Flyers to the world's trouble spots and testing the results in numerous studies as described in Chapter 5. One important test of the Yogic Flying program was conducted at Amherst, Massachusetts in 1979. It showed that when several thousand participants in the Yogic Flying program came together during a 40-day experimental period, motor vehicle deaths in Massachusetts were reduced 18.9%, and violent crime was reduced 10.1%.[3]

Numerous other experiments with similar results have been conducted in the last two decades, including a major evaluation of the program in 1993 in Washington, D.C. (see chart on next page). Dr. John Hagelin, a distinguished physicist and a principal exponent of Maharishi's programs, assembled an independent panel of more than 20 sociologists, criminologists, and members of the Washington, D.C. government and police department. At the outset of the study, and as it was being conducted, the independent panel advised on the study design, which aimed to reduce violence in the nation's capital. At the conclusion of the experiment, the panel analyzed the findings. The research results were striking. Over 4,000 Yogic Flyers participated in this assembly during the last two weeks of the two-month project. The research showed a decline in crime that ranged to approximately 20%, with the greatest decline occurring when the group of Yogic Flyers was largest at the end of the assembly, as was predicted. The researchers determined that the results could not be explained by factors other than the Yogic Flying program.[4]

Washington, D.C. Study

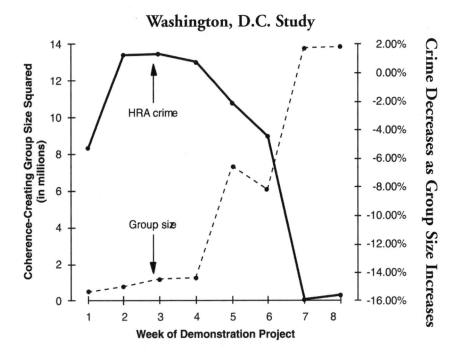

Despite the promising research, when most people think about ending terrorism, they think that a conventional military strength is necessary. Very few people appreciate the idea that collective consciousness can be an effective preventive force. However, scientists evaluating the research have been greatly impressed with the potential of Maharishi's programs.

Third Party Evaluations of the Research

Dr. Ted Robert Gurr, author of *Violence in America* and Distinguished University Professor in the Department of Government and Politics at the University of Maryland, one of the most respected scholars in the field of conflict analysis, says:

> In the studies that I have examined on the impact of [Maharishi's program] on conflict, I can find no methodological flaws, and the findings have been consistent across a

large number of replications in many different geographical and conflictual situations. As unlikely as the premise may sound, I think we have to take these studies seriously.

Dr. John Davies, from the University of Maryland's Center for International Development and Conflict Management, says "the research results are startling, but solid."

Dr. Juan Pascual-Leone, of York University in Ottawa, Canada, a member of the review board of the *Journal of Conflict Resolution* (which analyzed a major study of Maharishi's Vedic defense program), says simply, "the possibility is that we have made one of the most important discoveries of our time."

The Powerful Laws of Nature Supporting the Vedic Defense

How can consciousness be a powerful and effective force for peace? At subtle levels of the functioning of nature, modern physics identifies excitations of atoms and other small particles, which are extremely powerful in their effect. These findings are expressions of what appears to be a universal law of nature that can help us understand Maharishi's Vedic defense. *Scientists have discovered that the more subtle or fundamental the level of nature, the greater the potential power.*

In other words, the atomic level is understood by modern science to be more powerful than the molecular level, and the nuclear level is understood to be more powerful than the atomic level. This law of nature's functioning is understood by Vedic science to be applicable not just to the physical world, but also to the workings of consciousness. Because consciousness functions from the most subtle level of life—the transcendental field, which connects everyone and everything—it is through consciousness that we can actually have the most profound effect on human activity and the activity of nature. Maharishi's Vedic defense makes use of the powerful fluctuations of human consciousness in its most fundamental and, therefore, most powerful and coherent state.

Maharishi's Vedic Pandits

To overcome today's crisis in the U.S., Maharishi is assembling a core group of 8,000 U.S. Yogic Flyers and 500 Vedic *pandits* (trained experts from India) who will locate in Maharishi Vedic City, Iowa's newest city. Maharishi is also assembling a group of 40,000 of his Vedic pandits in India.

Maharishi's Vedic pandits are experts in consciousness who are able to achieve a highly coherent state of brain functioning through the Vedic defense procedures.

Maharishi's Vedic Pandits

Maharishi's pandits will practice the Transcendental Meditation and TM-Sidhi programs, including Yogic Flying, and also perform ancient Vedic procedures, known as *Yagya performances.* These procedures are traditionally understood to enliven the quality of peace in world consciousness, and to protect against war and terrorism. As set forth in Chapter 10, large

By tradition, the pandits live together in groups and perform the Vedic peace procedures virtually all day, every day.

groups of Maharishi's pandits will perform a particular Yagya from the

Vedic tradition, the *Ati Rudrabhisek Maha Yagya,* for many hours of the day. A *Maha Yagya* is a large Yagya performed by what is often many thousands of pandits. While smaller *Yagya performances* are performed for individuals in order to achieve business, personal, or health objectives, the Yagya for peace for a nation or even the world requires a great number of trained experts.

By tradition, the pandits live together in groups and perform the Vedic peace procedures virtually all day, every day; but it is not their reclusive lifestyle, or any religious faith, or particular belief system that is important. What is important are the specific techniques and procedures used by the pandits, and the perfect or near perfect functioning of their brains and nervous systems, which allows the pandits to function from the level of the transcendental field and give the mental procedures their effectiveness.

The Pandits and Yogic Flyers Perform the Vedic Peace Technologies in Groups at the Same Time

The reason for assembling the groups of Vedic pandits and Yogic Flyers is that their *peace-creating effect is greatly magnified when the groups practice their Yogic Flying and Yagya performances at the same time from the same approximate location.*

As explained more fully in Chapter 4, the laws of physics tell us that five loudspeakers placed next to one another and playing the same music in perfect synchrony will generate the volume of 25 loudspeakers placed at a distance—when the sound waves are in synchrony, their volume equals the square of the volume of waves not in synchrony. In the same way, when the 8,000 U.S. Yogic Flyers are assembled and practice their techniques from the same place at the same time, it has the effect on collective consciousness of 64 million Yogic Flyers (8,000 times 8,000) separately placed. The 40,000 pandits in the same vicinity in India are, therefore, predicted to have the effect that 1.6 billion pandits would have if they were dispersed throughout the world.

The programs of Maharishi's Vedic defense, when performed by a sufficiently large number of the Vedic experts, are a catalyst for the collective consciousness in a community to become more coherent and peaceful, preventing violence by anyone in the vicinity. The vicinity can be a community or even a nation or the entire world, depending on the sizes of the Vedic peace-creating groups. As previously explained, the group practice of the Vedic peace technologies causes not just a ripple effect, but produces a powerful wave of peace and coherence in the area.

Maharishi's Vedic Defense Is for Everyone

The crucial element in developing an immediate defense against terrorism is the creation of relatively large groups of Yogic Flyers and assembling large groups of Vedic pandits for the Yagya performances. However, an ideal world requires more than individual nations protecting themselves from terrorist activity and rogue nations through Maharishi's core groups. In the ideal scenario, the Transcendental Meditation program, Yogic Flying, and Yagya performances would be widely utilized in society, to allow everyone to develop their consciousness and contribute to international harmony. Maharishi explains that each of us contributes positively or negatively to the collective consciousness by radiating either a coherent or a stressful influence. If the collective consciousness is orderly and peaceful, it produces peace and prosperity in the society. If the collective consciousness is agitated and stressful, it produces disorder and violence.

The world is in a precarious state. We cannot depend on governments or the military to apply new paradigms for defending the nation against an unseen enemy of fanatics. As a result, Maharishi does not rely on government or the military to apply his Vedic defense. His is a citizen-based program—a program almost everyone can participate in to prevent acts of mass destruction in their locale.

Is It "Too Good to be True"?

Over the years Maharishi has not only taught the Vedic peace technologies, but has also encouraged a thorough scientific examination of his programs. In many instances the studies have been subjected to careful scrutiny by independent scientists through a process of peer review, and then were published in prominent journals. However, despite the scientific verification, not enough people in high places have seriously considered using this program to end conflict or to protect their nation from terrorism.

This is largely because the program introduces a new paradigm about how the world works and how terrorism can be prevented, and, therefore, lacks what is known as *verisimilitude,* the quality of being apparently true. A friend in advertising says that if you want advertising that reaches people, you have to make claims that are both true and that have the quality of appearing to be true. The research on the effectiveness of the Vedic peace technologies in preventing violence is solid. However, based on our everyday understandings, most people cannot imagine how a group of individuals participating in Maharishi's programs in one location could possibly influence those who may be miles or even hundreds or thousands of miles away, which is how the programs work. The common view of the world is an obsolete billiard ball perspective of how things work: one ball has to bang into another to have an effect, and individuals must have direct contact with others in order to influence them.

> The Vedic tradition explains what causes terrorism, how the victims are determined, and even how oncoming danger can be predicted.

Moreover, people who raise their eyebrows over Maharishi's programs having a peaceful effect on people in distance places, will likely have a similar reaction to other aspects of this new knowledge. The Vedic tradition explains what causes terrorism, how the victims are determined, and even how oncoming danger can be predicted. History tells us that new paradigms are not merely slow to be accepted. They are often vigorously attacked because they contradict the thinking of those who have built their lives on an entirely different view of how the world works.

In addition, a cultural divide inhibits any ready acceptance of Maharishi's programs. It is popularly safe to be open to new ideas and new products that come from General Electric or DuPont or Harvard. However, to someone who is unfamiliar with Maharishi, programs called *Yogic Flying* and *Transcendental Meditation* are quite a different thing in this country, even when these programs are backed by extensive scientific research and originate in the world's oldest, continuous tradition of knowledge.

While the main purpose of this book is to describe Maharishi's Vedic defense against terrorism, the book also offers a highly comforting view of life based on the Vedic perspective. Many people are thinking about the religious and philosophical implications of what occurred on September 11, 2001—the apparent randomness of life's events, how a merciful God can allow senseless killing, and the apparent injustice of bad things happening to good people. Maharishi explains why events like 9/11 occur, and shows how everything has its cause in the near or distant past, allowing us to see order and purpose in a world that might otherwise seem random and chaotic. This knowledge dispels the notion that preemptive wars can eliminate the terrorist threat, and offers a humane technology to deal with the current crisis. ■

TWO

Report of the 9/11 Commission: "We Are Not Safe"

"Because of offensive actions against al-Qaeda since 9/11, and defensive actions to improve homeland security, we believe we are safer today. But we are not safe."

The 9/11 Report of the National Commission on Terrorist Attacks Upon the United States

A Steady Growth in Terrorism

Terrorism is steadily growing in most parts of the world. While the Middle East is still the world's hotspot for terrorist activities, large-scale attacks in recent years have occurred, for example, on the Bali Islands (killing 202 people in a nightclub), in the Tokyo subway system, in Russia, the latter being the September 2004 Chechen attacks that downed two Russian planes and massacred hundreds at the Beslan school, and, of course, in the U.S. in 2001. *Increasingly, the trend in terrorism is toward attacks against the United States and its supporters.*

The FBI defines terrorism as the use or threat of violence in furtherance of political, social, or religious objectives. During the 1970s, there were 8,014 terrorist incidents, increasing to 31,426 incidents during the 1980s, and 27,087 incidents in the first six years of the 1990s. The number of deaths from worldwide terrorist incidents grew from 4,798 deaths in the 1970s, to 70,859 deaths in the 1980s, and approximately 52,000 deaths in the first six years of the 1990s.[1]

While there have been more terrorist incidents in other countries, Americans abroad have been the targets of the largest and most destructive attacks over the past 30 years, and recently Americans are being targeted within the U.S. The attacks on Americans have included the bombing of the U.S. barracks at the Beirut airport in 1983 (241 marines and 58 French paratroopers killed), the destruction of Pan American flight 103 over Lockerbie, Scotland in 1988 (270 deaths), the bombing of the Murrah Federal Building in Oklahoma City in 1995 (168 deaths), the car bombings of embassies in Nairobi and Dar es Salaam in 1998 (224 deaths), and the attack of September 11, 2001 (3,030 total deaths).

Before September 11, 2001, however, the majority of the terrorist attacks in the U.S. were from *domestic* sources—right wingers, left wingers, and special interest groups (the extreme fringes of animal rights, pro-life, antinuclear, and other movements)—and these attacks did not threaten mass destruction. Now, the threats are also from well-organized or state-backed militant groups overseas, and we know that mass destruction is possible.

The principal factors in the growing anti-American sentiment in the world, and especially in Muslim countries, include America's support of Israel, Western immorality, Western materialism, and a perceived godlessness in the West. Ahmed Al-Hafedh, a young citizen of Lebanon who has studied in the United States, told us:

> The image in the West is that terrorists are young men who are recruited and brainwashed, and who become cold-bloodedly programmed. But that's not the case. It's an act of rage and hopelessness. They don't need to be recruited, they volunteer. Of course, where they are wrong is in choosing violence in the first place, and in putting all citizens in the same basket as the leaders. But it is hard for a tortured mind to be able to see through all of this.

There is widely divergent thinking on who is at fault in the Middle East conflict. However, it is clear that much like the legendary battles of the Hatfields and McCoys, in the battles between Israelis and Palestinians both sides have been blinded by their hatred as the conflict has escalated. It was awful the first time Palestinians switched from throwing rocks to shooting at Israelis. Then shootings became common. We were shocked by suicide bombings until they, too, became routine. It was shocking the first time Israel used F-16s against Palestinian targets, but now this is also a common tactic, as Israel and Palestine continue their retaliations. Each believes that God is on their side and that they have no choice but to up the ante or at least match it, and the horrific has become the routine.

The Risks Inherent in Our Response

Can America avoid a cycle of attacks and retaliations like those between the Israelis and Palestinians? Several weeks after the September 11 attacks in 2001, Congressman Jim Leach spoke at a political rally in Burlington, Iowa. One of the most thoughtful members of Congress, Leach expressed the conventional wisdom in Washington. He said that in dealing with terrorism, the objective is a "modulated response" that retaliates against only the attackers and those who harbor them. If the response is overbroad, or if nothing is done, Leach said, it invites further attacks.

However, in a modulated response against terrorists and those who support them, who do we attack after the Taliban, al-Qaeda, and Iraq? Should we attack the Islamic Jihad, the Muslim Brotherhood, Hezballah, as well as the nations of Iran, Syria, the Sudan, North Korea, and others who may be giving aid to terrorist activity or developing nuclear weapons? Because any nation's ability to defend against a terrorist attack is limited, preemptive attacks or "preventive" wars are the principal U.S. strategy in the war on terrorism, and preemption inevitably results in the killing of many innocent civilian men, women, and children. In seeking a modulated response, there are endless possibilities for mistakes in both air and land campaigns. Experience shows that distinguishing between civilians and the enemy can be impossible, that all sides ignore human rights in war, and killing or degrading those we oppose provokes retaliation. In the Abu Ghraib prison scandal, the U.S. is now reduced to arguing that its atrocities aren't as bad as the other side's.

> "[We] have no way of telling whether we are winning or losing the war on terror."
>
> *Donald Rumsfeld, in his 10/16/2003 memorandum on the global war on terror*

What happens when civilians are killed? Many of the Iraqis who lost family members over the past 10 years hated Sadaam Hussein; now, unfortunately, many of these people also hate the United States. An Associated Press report on the killing of U.S. soldiers in Iraq (November 25, 2003 from Mosul, Iraq) illustrates the perspective of typical Iraqis. Abdullah al-Mulla, who works in a gas station in Iraq, said, "If an American came to my house at night and took me away in front of my children, I would have to take revenge." The Associated Press story explained that the Middle East Arab culture is steeped in traditions of a powerful code of honor and vendetta. Revenge killing is considered a normal, moral act. Mr. al-Mulla said, "The Americans kill people by mistake and then apologize the next day. This doesn't work here."

Kulwant Singh, a Major General in the Indian Army and an expert in counter-terrorism, recently told audiences in our hometown of Fairfield, Iowa, about a young Pakistani terrorist, a well-known soccer star, who tried to take a cyanide capsule when he was captured by the Indian army. When interrogated and asked why he wanted to commit suicide, he said that

> "[S]upport for the United States has plummeted... by 2003 polls showed that the bottom has fallen out of support for America in most of the Muslim world."

if he died after being caught, it would increase the hatred of thousands of individuals who might now only loosely support his fight against India.

Are We Safer Since 9/11?

In the face of growing anti-American sentiment, have we become a safer nation due to the expenditure of billions of dollars for defense and attacks on al-Queda and Iraq? Secretary of Defense Donald Rumsfeld, in his October 16, 2003 memorandum on the global war on terror, stated that we have no way of telling whether we are winning or losing the war on terror. He said:

> The questions I posed to combatant commanders this week were: Are we winning or losing the global war on terror? Today, we lack the metrics to know if we are winning or

losing the global war on terror. Are we capturing, killing, or deterring and dissuading more terrorists every day than the madrassas and the radical clerics are recruiting, training and deploying against us?

Rumsfeld's criteria for determining if we are winning or losing the war is based on the number of radicals being recruited and trained, a process made far easier today as a result of the unprecedented growth of anti-American sentiment around the globe, and especially in Muslim countries.

A September 13, 2004 report in *Time* magazine ("Islam Around the World") states:

Though precise figures are impossible to pinpoint, the number of Muslims espousing radical beliefs is growing, according to Western analysts and intelligence agencies. Many Muslims say the global war on terrorism and the U.S. presence in Iraq have fueled perceptions that Islam is under attack.

The *9/11 Report of the National Commission on Terrorist Attacks Upon the United States* acknowledges that "support for the United States has plummeted," and that by 2003 polls showed "that the bottom has fallen out of support for America in most of the Muslim world."[2] Immediately after 9/11, polls in Islamic countries showed that approximately half the people of those countries had a favorable opinion of the United States. Now, however, the situation has worsened dramatically. Egypt, for example, the *9/11 Report* states, has been a long-time ally of the United States and has received more U.S. aid in the past 20 years than any other country. However, today only 15% of Egypt's population have a favorable view of the United States. In Saudi Arabia, the figure is 12%. In Indonesia the figure is 15%. Negative views of the U.S. among Muslims, which were previously limited to countries in the Middle East, has now spread to Muslim nations everywhere. According to the *9/11 Report*, a climate of fear has been created where two-thirds of Muslims are either fearful or somewhat fearful that the U.S. may attack them. In this environment, does anyone really believe there are not more terrorists today than before 9/11?

In assessing the nation's safety, in addition to the number of radicals, what must concern us most is the potential for a nuclear attack or large scale chemical or biological attack. It is estimated that a nuclear device of a size that could fit in a minivan would destroy

> "...there may be tens of thousands of nuclear weapons that can be purchased on the black market. These weapons fit into a minivan...."
>
> *Dr. Graham Allison, director of the Belfer Center for Science and International Affairs at Harvard University*

everything within a mile of the blast. Dropped in New York City where the Twin Towers stood, it would have resulted in the complete annihilation of the southern tip of Manhattan, with buildings for several miles reduced to rubble, and the deaths of several hundred thousand individuals. Is such an attack really possible?

In an interview with *Nova* in February 2003, Dr. Graham Allison, director of the Belfer Center for Science and International Affairs at Harvard University and former assistant Secretary of Defense under President Clinton, stated that while manufacturing nuclear weapons from scratch involves massive production facilities, there may be tens of thousands of nuclear weapons that can be purchased on the black market. These weapons fit into a minivan and can be moved through relatively porous borders into the Middle East or onto cargo ships or planes for transport to the U.S. With 500 million people crossing our borders every year and only 5% of cargo containers being inspected, Dr. Allison believes a nuclear attack in the U.S. is more likely than not. He said:

> Why didn't 9/11 happen before? The answer is we were fortunate. I would not say it's inevitable that there will be a nuclear terror attack (although Warren Buffet, who is a pretty good judge of risk, at least when it comes to investing, says he thinks it's essentially inevitable). But I would say it is highly likely.

Homeland Security

In view of the extreme nature of the terrorist threat, can a reorganization of government and increased expenditures on conventional strategies protect the nation from the unseen fanatic? With the new Homeland Security Department, the U.S. now has a 170,000-person force from 22 agencies with a streamlined mission to defend us against terrorism. The National Commission on Terrorist Attacks recommends an even further reorganization of government to build a unified effort through a national Counter Terrorism Center and a National Intelligence Director. But neither centralized operations nor billions of dollars spent on conventional or high tech defense strategies can stop a terrorist in a minivan from finding some populated area to detonate his device.

In defending against terrorism, the nation will have to defend against potentially hundreds of thousands of individuals who would do us harm, including homegrown terrorists. There is a growing threat from domestic terrorists such as The World Church of the Creator with its hateful literature, the Aryan Nation, the Southern States Alliance of militia men, and hundreds of other groups. Domestic terrorists, while not center stage today, have been the source of more attacks in the U.S. than those by overseas agents, and the magnitude of the domestic threat cannot be ignored. Dennis Beauregard, Brigadier General of the Southern States Alliance, was arrested several years ago for breaking into a National Guard armory to steal weapons. His plan was to blow up the Crystal River nuclear plant in Florida, which would have made Florida uninhabitable for 30 years.

No one says we should ignore conventional and high tech approaches to defending ourselves against terrorism, but none of them can protect everyone within a given location. Most people recognize that there are just too many possibilities for breaches in security. International terrorists are not concerned about direct combat against large forces. They simply seek the vulnerabilities that exist in urban areas and near power plants, municipal water supplies, and other such targets. Washington is, therefore, led to preemption as its major weapon in the war against terrorism.

Are Preemptive Strikes a Necessary Evil?

The conventional wisdom offers numerous arguments for and against a preemptive approach to fighting terrorism. Professor Alan Kuperman, of the Johns Hopkins University School of Advanced International Studies, offered his views in "Preemption: Should USA Punch First?" published in *USA Today* on November 12, 2002. Professor Kuperman argued that a first-strike strategy is likely to backfire by actually causing the wars it seeks to prevent. He says that our preemptive attacks encourage other states to launch similar first strikes, with potentially disastrous results. Professor Kuperman reminds us that the use of military force usually spawns opposition, and that, historically, nearly all nations undermined their power by abusing it in a preemptive manner. In our communications with Professor Kuperman, he also pointed out that the U.S. war against Iraq is really not what would classically be termed a preemptive attack. Preemptive attacks are launched in anticipation of *an imminent attack* from an opponent. The war against Iraq is more precisely referred to as a "preventive war," meaning an attack against an opponent that is weak to forestall a future attack when it becomes stronger.

In any event, Professor Kuperman's views are just part of the story. A contrary view on preemptive or preventive strikes is offered by Robert Andrews, a former CIA officer, and former deputy Assistant Secretary of Defense. In his article in the same issue of *USA Today* on November 12, 2002, he justifies preemption as a necessary evil and argues that if Mohammed Atta and the others who piloted the 9/11 attacks had access to nuclear, chemical, or biological weapons, they would have used them. Mr. Andrews concludes that preemption is necessary against enemies who cannot be contained, and who would use weapons of mass destruction against the U.S. Mr. Andrews argues that while we cannot know for certain the consequences of our preemptive policy, earlier preemptive actions have not unleashed retaliatory attacks. He cites as examples Israel's 1981 attack on Saddam Hussein's Osirak nuclear reactor, which did not result in a large-scale Iraqi attack, and prior U.S. preemptive actions in Grenada, Panama, and Haiti, which also did not result in a major reaction from these countries.

The Vedic Perspective

Is there any way of knowing what the consequences will be from preemptive or "preventive" attacks that kill civilians as well as would-be terrorists? According to the Vedic perspective, there are *inevitable* consequences from attacks that cause killing. Maharishi has said many times that killing is sinful, and that the killers will themselves be destroyed. Maharishi is speaking literally. He explains that whatever good or bad a person does comes back in kind. This is called *karma* in the Vedic literature, and like the expression, "As you sow, so shall you reap," or "measure for measure" in Judaism's Talmud, this concept explains why bad things happen to good people. Karma, according to the Vedic tradition, is inevitable—an *immutable* law of nature.

For most of us, however, there is nothing inevitable about karma, based on everyday experience. We know that those who commit violent acts often go unpunished, and young people can become victims of tragic events or die from some terrible disease. We observe many injustices in life, leading some to question the existence of God, or to accept the notion that bad acts occur without reason, that life is a matter of chance, and that justice comes only in heaven or hell, or not at all.

On the Larry King television show in May 2002, Maharishi was asked about tragic deaths in the context of the attack on the World Trade Center on September 11, 2001.

> Maharishi: In the process of evolution, the body lasts for some time and then one takes another body and takes another body and takes another body. Everyone has to go... sometime or the other. And the basic principle about going or surviving is that no one—now listen to me—no one is responsible for giving any difficulty or any pleasure to anyone. Problems or successes, they all are the results of our own actions. Karma. The philosophy of action is that no one else is the giver of peace or happiness. One's own karma, one's own actions, are responsible to bring either happiness or success or whatever.

King: If someone treats me harshly, if someone shoots me or kills you, or harms a baby... how was the victim a participant in that other than being in the wrong place at the wrong time?

Maharishi: He [the wrongdoer] is the carrier of my own influence. "As you sow, so shall you reap" is a very old proverb of mankind. "As you sow, so shall you reap." Sometime you may have killed that man; and then sometime, now, it comes on to you.

King: Ah.

Maharishi: What we have done, the result of that comes to us whenever it comes: either today, tomorrow, hundred years later, hundred lives later.... Whatever, whatever. It's our own karma. That is why that philosophy is in every religion, Killing is sin. Killing is sin in every religion. Whosoever sins, whosoever kills, it doesn't matter. It's a sin.

King: Right.

Maharishi: And sin in the will of God is a punishable offense. Because when you kill some man, what you are killing? You are killing the cosmic potential within the individual. Individual is cosmic. Individual potential of life is cosmic potential. Individual is divine, deep inside; transcendental experience awakens that divinity in man. And when you kill a man, you deprive him of that birthright of his.

King: What a wonderful way to look at it.

Maharishi: The human right to live divinity.

Maharishi has also explained how the accumulated wrong actions of individuals can produce reactions that affect entire areas or regions. For example, war in a particular region results from a buildup of extreme levels of wrongdoing, violence, and stress in that region. The collective stress in a particular area erupts into mass violence. Mass destruction from a terrorist attack occurs in a particular area as a result of the collective past wrongdoing in that region, and everyone in the area is affected.

Speaking at a news conference on December 11, 2002, Maharishi gave the following answers to the questions posed to him about preemptive approaches.

> Karma, according to the Vedic tradition, is inevitable—an immutable law of nature.

Question: Maharishi, this is a rather pressing question from a military writer in Washington, D.C. The top story in today's *Washington Post* is that the Bush administration has announced it will use preemptive military and covert force, before an enemy unleashes weapons of mass destruction. And also that the U.S. is willing to retaliate with nuclear weapons or chemical or biological weapons against acts on U.S. soil or against U.S. troops overseas. The *Washington Post* writes that this breaks with 50 years of U.S. strategy based on deterrence and containment. This preemption doctrine favors taking on hostile states before they can strike.... But the question is, Bush's use of preemptive force is obviously an attempt to prevent a larger war with a smaller war. Would Maharishi please comment on this strategy and whether he has a better alternative?

Maharishi: I have an alternative in one word. Prevention. Vedic defense is not in offense. Offense obviously is not defense. Offense is not defense. You can be offensive to someone; he or his friends will be offensive to you. So by offending someone, you can't defend yourself. By offending someone, you don't defend yourself.

There is a country proverb in the Vedic field: it says, *Kamsakat Gutsajagya* or "Strength less makes anger more." So anger is on the basis of less strength. When you can't achieve something, you flare up, you become angry. So when someone has the responsibility of saving his family, saving his country, and he doesn't know anything in order to prevent the enemy, then he can only plunge into fire. Plunging into fire is a defeat of first grade, that you don't know how to defend yourself.

Heyam Dukham Anagatam ["Prevent the birth of an enemy" or, "Avert the danger that has not yet come"]. This is Vedic defense. Vedic means pertaining to knowledge. So defense on the basis of knowledge offers prevention, prevention. Prevent the birth of an enemy. If you can't prevent the birth of an enemy, then you are your own enemy.... It sounds highly philosophical, but it is realistic. Defense is only prudent, defense is only wise in disallowing the enemy.

Now you see the enemy is somewhere, somewhere. And then from his home, from his country, he just marches, marches, and then comes to your border. When he comes to your border, then you begin to shoot him. Would it not be wise to shoot him when he is half way to your border? Would it not be still wiser to shoot him when he starts from home? Would it not be wiser to shoot down his desire to start attacking you? This is prevention. Attack him, but attack him at the source of his desire to harm you.

Now, how to do that thing? What is [there] within your power to disallow the birth of your enemy? Now you have to go deep into the cause of your enemy. Why the enemy is wanting to attack you? Why this desire? Why his desire to attack you? To cut the whole story short there is an expression in the Vedic literature, in the field of knowledge, the expression is *Sukhasya Dukhtsya Nagopidathal.* It is a great expression. The happiness or misery, nobody delivers to you. It appears that he did this good, and he did this wrong. It appears to be. But nobody delivers to you anything good or anything bad. He only reacts to your good or your bad. You do something bad, and someone will echo it back on you. You do something good, and someone will echo back on you some good.

If our future is a result of our own past actions, it raises the question of whether, and to what extent, our future is predetermined and whether we have free will. The answer from Maharishi is that there is both predetermination and free will. We had free will in the past, which created influences that have already ripened into some events, and which will ripen into events to come. At the same time, each one of us has the experience that we can determine what we want to do, although we often find that circumstances may compel us in a particular direction. As an example, a car may be built of good materials and be well designed and well constructed. This permits the car to last for 20 years. However, it must be properly maintained. Similarly, the individual's past actions result in a certain physiology at birth, which will influence the lifespan and events in life, but the physiology must also be properly maintained or the lifespan may be shortened.

What happens to us in life is a result of the interaction of our past and our present. Maharishi explains that if people speak ill of us and misunderstand our actions, or if things just do not go well for us, it has been caused by something we have done in the present life or in an earlier life. If bad things are happening, then they are a result of our past wrong action—our own creation coming back to us in the present. "As you sow, so shall you reap" is a law of nature, according to the Vedic perspective. It may work quickly resulting in reactions from those in the immediate surroundings, or the consequences may be delivered tomorrow or in another lifetime. In his book, *The Science of Being and Art of Living*, Maharishi explains:

> If you act to someone in a certain way, he in turn will react to you in a similar way. If he does not react to you, then nature will bring to you a similar type of reaction. If you hurt someone, even if he, himself, does not react, other agencies of nature will bring the reaction of your behavior to you....

> If you hate, the surroundings begin to hate you. If the surroundings hate you, do not blame the surroundings, blame your own inner conscience.... If you are clear in conscience and loving, kind and virtuous to your fellow men...and yet there is still something wrong in your surroundings, then take it as it comes; it is the result of some action in the past. If you retaliate, you are brought to the level of the wrong. Rather let the wrong be a drop in the ocean of your virtue.[3]

The Vedic tradition of knowledge clearly states that we are responsible for our own destiny, and nothing occurs by chance. Instead of a worldview that sees random events, chaos, and unexplainable circumstances, the Vedic tradition describes an almost unimaginable order in creation, and a Creator of unbounded intelligence and kindness, dispensing perfect justice. "It is the kindness of God that He gave unlimited freedom to man," says Maharishi. Everyone is given the freedom to do good or bad, but it is a great misunderstanding, Maharishi explains, to think that we can do bad things and that God will just forgive us.

> While the karma of previous wrongdoing brings consequences in the future, the consequences can at least be mitigated through the Vedic peace technologies.

If there are inevitable consequences from previous wartime excesses and acts of terrorism, then the Western world's actions must also result in extreme consequences that may be coming back to us now. In the late 1940s, the British chiefs of staff decided to bomb the centers of key German cities, killing 300,000 Germans, most of them civilians, and seriously wounding another 780,000. The U.S. also rejected options to warn the Japanese by dropping an atomic bomb in the Sea of Japan, or in outlying rice paddies, or by detonating the bomb high above Tokyo. Instead, we decided to terrorize Japan into submission by dropping the bombs on civilians in Hiroshima and Nagasaki when we were already decimating Japan with fire bombs.

Former Secretary of Defense Robert S. McNamara recently described the fire bombing of Japanese cities in the film *The Fog of War*. McNamara said:

> I was in General Le May's command in Guam in March, 1945. In that single night, we burned to death 100,000 Japanese civilians in Tokyo: men, women and children. I was part of a mechanism that in a sense recommended it [the fire bombing of Japan].
>
> The issue is not incendiary bombs. The issue is in order to win

a war, should you kill 100,000 people in one night by fire bombing or any other way. General Le May's answer would be clearly "yes." He went on from Tokyo to fire bomb other cities. 58% of Yokohama. Yokohama is roughly the size of Cleveland. 58% of Cleveland [we] destroyed. Tokyo is roughly the size of New York. 51% of New York destroyed. [We destroyed] 99% of the equivalent of Chattanooga, which is Toyama. 40% of the equivalent of Los Angeles, which is Nagaya.

This was all done before the dropping of the atomic bombs.... Killing 50–90% of the people in 67 Japanese cities and then bombing them with two nuclear bombs is not proportional in the minds of some people to the objectives we were trying to achieve....

General Le May said if we had lost the war we would have all been prosecuted as war criminals. And I think he's right. He and I would say we were behaving as war criminals.

The Role We Must Take

Maharishi has stated many times that governments and those who have significant resources have a responsibility to take action to protect themselves and those in their communities, yet he warns that if the U.S., or any country, takes on the role of the destroyer, it will itself be destroyed.

Maharishi is not advocating any lessening of emphasis on the conventional methods of defense. He understands that it is necessary to enhance the readiness of the nation to respond to biological, chemical, and genetic warfare, but he also understands that no conventional approach can be a complete defense against a bomb in a suitcase or minivan. And while the karma of previous wrongdoing brings consequences in the future, the consequences can at least be mitigated through the Vedic peace technologies. In other words, if a blow is coming as a result of past wrongdoing, it can be made to be a glancing blow by enlivening the peaceful aspects of nature through Maharishi's Yogic Flying program, and through Vedic performances known as *Yagyas*. The Yagya performances directly address any dangers that may be on the horizon—those that are coming toward us as a reaction to our own past wrongdoing (see Chapters 9 and 10).

Maharishi, therefore, is seeking an increased enrollment of Yogic Flyers in his universities and in other Vedic peace-creating facilities being constructed in each nation (Peace Palaces), as well as an increase in the number of Vedic pandits trained to perform the Yagyas for peace. These will be core groups practicing the Vedic peace technologies to change the collective consciousness in their area. For governments choosing to assist this approach, Maharishi has proposed that they add a prevention wing to the military, which would train a very small percentage of the military in Vedic defense. The size of the group necessary to significantly change the collective consciousness has been found to be only the square root of one percent of the population to be affected. Therefore, 8,000 Yogic Flyers and Vedic pandits performing their program together have the effect of 64 million Yogic Flyers performing their program separately, and they can influence a population of 6.4 billion people. See Chapter 5.

Dwight Eisenhower once said he believed "people in the long run are going to do more to promote peace than our governments." Eisenhower said, "people want peace so much that one of these days governments had better get out of the way and let them have it." Maharishi's approach to preventing terrorism echoes this sentiment. His approach is not dependent on governments, which may have many motivations for their preemptive or preventive attacks, and who typically ignore strategies from outside the mainstream in their effort to remain popular with the masses. ∎

THREE

The Principles of Vedic Science at the Basis of Maharishi's Vedic Defense

The Vedic Literature Is Not Man-Made Knowledge

How seriously should we take the Vedic perspective on terrorism? Is it just one opinion to be evaluated among others? As previously indicated, the knowledge that is the source of the Vedic defense is part of the oldest and most complete records of human knowledge and human development. This knowledge was obtained much differently from the manner in which knowledge is typically gained in the West. Maharishi explains that Vedic science holds that there are really two methods of gaining knowledge, the objective method, which uses trial and error, observation, and experiment, and is similar to the methodologies of Western science; and the subjective method, a method of gaining knowledge through the direct insights or cognitions of enlightened Vedic sages.

According to Maharishi, the Vedic knowledge is *Nitya* (eternal) and *Apaurusheya* (not man-made), and was *cognized* by enlightened Vedic sages. This means that the knowledge came to the enlightened mind in a complete form, ready to be expressed orally or written down for the benefit of others. The Veda and Vedic literature are not, therefore, a product of trial and error, or of intellectual debate, or the judgments and evaluations that are part of the way knowledge is presently obtained in an academic setting. The knowledge in the Vedic texts is gained as a result of direct experiences or understandings that come not just as a vague hunch, but in explicit detail.

To the Vedic sages, the subjective means of gaining knowledge through direct experience is actually held to be the most reliable means of gaining knowledge, and, surprisingly, this may be the perspective of the greatest thinkers in the West. Newton and Einstein, while they obviously gained important knowledge through sensory perception and the methods of conventional education, are probably best known for discoveries that resulted from direct insights (i.e., the subjective method). For example, both Newton, in comprehending the laws of gravity, and Einstein, in discovering the laws of special relativity, reported that the knowledge came as a sudden insight or direct cognition.

Within the Vedic tradition are specific procedures to develop an *enlightened* state of consciousness. As a result of a vast body of scientific research, we now appreciate that the state of enlightenment is not a mystical or religious state, but results from neurophysiological refinement leading to total brain development. In this higher state of human development, the nervous system can be used as a kind of microscope to explore the innermost Self, referred to in the Vedic literature as *Atma*. The enlightened Vedic sages explored the fluctuations within their own settled states of consciousness and had direct insights into the nature of consciousness, as well as the nature of the world.

The classical Vedic meditation, which Maharishi has revived in the world today as the Transcendental Meditation technique, allowed the Vedic sages to experience the most settled state of consciousness, pure consciousness. Through advanced Vedic procedures, known today as the TM-Sidhi program, which includes Yogic Flying, the sages were able to function from that least excited state of mind. They came to know that pure, settled state as the underlying field that is the source of both mind and matter. Maharishi explains that it is *possible to influence everyone from this level of consciousness* because everyone and everything is linked together by the same underlying field. Maharishi refers to this field as the Unified Field of Natural Law or the transcendental field.

Everyone Is Interconnected

Modern science has come to the same conclusions as Vedic science concerning the interconnectedness of everything at fundamental levels. Initially, classical physics viewed the world as composed of solid bits of matter, which affected each other mainly through direct physical contact (the Newtonian model). Psychologists and sociologists then developed similar models, which pictured individuals as wholly separate, and capable of influencing others only through direct contact. But while matter is discrete and separate on some levels, twentieth-century developments in quantum mechanics and quantum field theory have shown that *connectedness* is found at deeper levels of nature, where the characteristics of nature are expressed throughout underlying fields. Quantum physics describes *everything* in the universe as connected, as part of a continuum. Physicist David Bohm, who wrote a classic textbook on quantum physics, conducted landmark research showing the interconnectedness of small particles at subtle levels of creation. He

> Maharishi explains that it is possible to influence everyone from this level of consciousness because everyone and everything is linked together by the same underlying field.

explains that individual things may be separate at what he calls the *explicate level*, but there is an underlying *implicate* level, and the implicate level and the explicate level blend into each other.

Dr. John Hagelin, the winner in 1992 of the prestigious Kilby Award in physics, has extended this concept in describing a precise and detailed correspondence between the field of consciousness, *Atma*, and the latest theories of modern physics known as "superstring theories." These theories have satisfied Einstein's dream of discovering one unified field that unites all the forces of nature. Physics has now really come to the same understanding as Vedic science—that all of creation is interconnected through fluctuations of underlying, *continuous fields* which pervade the universe (refer to illustration on page 9). By his achievement in correlating the most fundamental field of physics with the most fundamental field of consciousness, Dr. Hagelin has brought physics into a new dimension, allowing physicists to have new insights based on the most ancient understandings about consciousness.

Dr. Hagelin also developed a model for understanding the mechanics of Maharishi's Vedic defense programs, in particular how large groups of Yogic Flyers can create coherence in the collective consciousness of a nation or the world. One basic principle of nature, well understood by physics, allows Yogic Flyers to influence those at a distance in the "vicinity" of the Yogic Flying group. As previously explained, a central broadcasting station, as an example of this principle, propagates electronic waves through the electro-

magnetic field, permitting receivers at a distance to show televised images. This principle is known in physics as *action at a distance*. This is a funda-mental attribute of fields, through which an event at one location can exert an influence that carries information through the field. This results in an almost immediate long-range effect (the central broadcasting station sends an instantaneous signal to everyone with a TV in the area). Viewed from this perspective, Dr. Hagelin says that the coherence generated by the Yogic Flyers produces a coherent effect on the society at large because consciousness also displays field-like attributes and thus can generate field effects, including *action at a distance*. The human brain has the capacity to be both a transmitter and a receiver, radiating or receiving subtle influ-ences through the field of consciousness. When those involved in the Transcendental Meditation and TM-Sidhi programs experience *Atma*, pure consciousness, the deepest level of consciousness, they radiate a soci-ety-wide influence of *harmony and coherence*. Like a central broadcasting station, Yogic Flyers radiate a signal to everyone, because everyone has a receiv-er (the human brain). Dr. Hagelin says that since all other natural phenomena produce field effects and action at a dis-tance, the field effects of consciousness should not be surprising unless we are prepared to adopt a view of life that

states that somehow consciousness is fundamentally different from all other natural phenomena.

The Constitution of the Universe

Maharishi tells us that the Vedic sounds comprising the Vedic literature are the most basic vibrations in nature, constituting what amounts to a blueprint for the functioning of the universe. Maharishi describes one particular branch of the Vedic knowledge, known as *Rik Veda*, as being the *Constitution of the Universe*. We don't normally think of the universe as having a constitution, but all laws, whether man-made laws or nature's laws, must originate

> The sounds in the Vedic literature have their set sequences, and one traditional role of the Vedic pandits is to recite the Vedic sounds in their proper sequence. This maintains order in the individual and in the society as a whole.

from some underlying, unifying principles. Just as the constitution of every nation represents the most fundamental level of laws governing the nation, the sounds or frequencies of the Rik Veda, as the Constitution of the Universe, represent the most fundamental level of Natural Law, and the ultimate source of the order and harmony displayed throughout the creation. This level of nature, Maharishi explains, is lively in the intelligence of every grain of creation.

One example might help in explaining how the Rik Veda could be the blueprint of the universe, and the basis of all order and harmony in life. Due to parallel laws of nature found at different levels of life, our DNA acts as a blueprint for our body in much the same way as the Vedic sounds act as a blueprint for the universe. As the body's blueprint, the DNA is present in virtually every cell of the body, just as the Rik Veda frequencies and vibrations are present in every grain of creation (and, therefore, underlie the DNA). The information in the DNA is also encoded in a sequence of specific chemicals called nucleotides, in the same manner as the Rik Veda, and all the Vedic literature, is composed of a set sequence of sounds. Within the DNA are specific regions that contain the set of instructions, or memory, to insure that the DNA information is expressed in a precise, sequential manner so that the innumerable parts of our body function in a balanced and harmonious way. When the DNA is not expressed in a precise sequential manner, it can cause cells to behave abnormally and even to become cancerous. Similarly, the sounds in the Vedic literature have their set sequences, and one traditional role of the Vedic pandits is to recite the Vedic sounds in their proper sequence. This maintains order in the individual and in the society as a whole. Maharishi's Vedic tradition holds that disordered and unhealthy conditions occur in society when the Vedic sounds are not kept lively through the precise recitation of the sounds by the Vedic pandits.

The Vedic Sounds Are at the Basis of the Human Physiology

One recent finding of historic proportions helps to illustrate how the Vedic sounds underlie the human physiology and are the blueprint of the material world. Dr. Tony Nader, a physician with a Ph.D. in brain science from MIT, discovered that the human physiology has a form, structure, and function that precisely mirrors the form, structure, and function of the Vedic literature. When Dr. Nader looked at the structure of the Vedic literature, he noted a remarkable parallel to what he knew to be the structure of the human physiology.

In his book, *Human Physiology: Expression of Veda and the Vedic Literature,* Dr. Nader gives a detailed analysis of how all aspects of the physiology, from the DNA to the entire physiology, correspond to specific branches of the Vedic literature.

In one example Dr. Nader correlates the section of Vedic literature on Yoga with the structure of the human brain. The section on Yoga contains four chapters that correspond precisely to the four lobes of the human brain. Within each of the four chapters on Yoga are the Vedic sounds in the form of Sanskrit verses, and the number of verses is exactly equal to the number of folds (called *gyri*) in that particular section of the brain. In other words, the 55 verses in the first chapter of the book on Yoga correspond to the 55 sets of folds in the occipital lobe and so on, with each of the 195 verses in the book of Yoga corresponding to each of the 195 sets of folds in the brain, with each verse even corresponding to a particular fold, the longer verses, for example, corresponding to the longer folds.[1]

Correspondence of Brain with Yoga Sutras

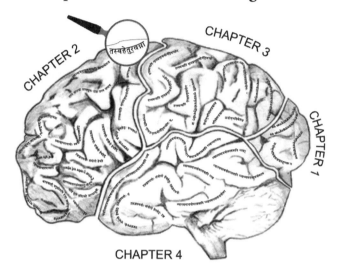

CHAPTER 2   CHAPTER 3   CHAPTER 1

CHAPTER 4

As one more example, the hypothalamus has eight regions, with four nuclei in each, which correspond to the eight chapters, each with four sections of *Vykaran*, another of the branches of the Vedic literature. Dr. Nader actually found a similar remarkable correspondence between *all* the principal parts of the human nervous system and the principal texts of the Vedic literature.

As suggested by Dr. Nader's research, the one-to-one correspondence of the Vedic literature with the human physiology is not just some cosmic coincidence. Maharishi has explained that the Vedic sounds in the Vedic literature are themselves the vibrations and frequencies that give rise to the human physiology, as well as everything else in the world, promoting harmony in the functioning of the physiology and harmony in society.

Maharishi considers Dr. Nader's discovery of the Veda and the Vedic literature in the human physiology as the greatest scientific discovery of this age. The discovery, for example, has extraordinary medical applications. It gives us a guide to which sounds of the Vedic literature, when recited or listened to, can reorder or heal the corresponding part of the physiology by enlivening the fundamental frequencies responsible for that part of the body. Similarly the Vedic literature tells us which sounds, when recited, correct disorder in society through the Yagya performances, as described more fully in Chapter 10. The Vedic sounds can have this effect because the Vedic sounds are themselves the laws of nature that govern the entire cosmos. Because of the greatness of his discoveries, Maharishi has crowned Dr. Nader as Raja (king) Raam, king of Maharishi's newly created Global Country of World Peace. This is not a country defined by geographical boundaries, but one whose sovereignty is in the domain of consciousness. The Global Country of World Peace aims to bring a true sovereignty to every nation by supporting every national constitution through the Vedic strategies to create health, harmony, and prosperity. Dr. Nader says:[2]

> The laws of nature are...in Vedic terms, the *Vrittis* of *Atma*—reverberations of the Self—our own simplest form of awareness. Maharishi has shown that all the laws of nature are available in a verbal form in the sounds, syllables, and verses of the Vedic Literature. Under Maharishi's guidance, it has [also] been possible to scientifically show that the human physiology is an exact replica of the...Veda and the Vedic Literature. Our own body reflects precisely the structure and functions, divisions and subdivisions, of the Vedic Literature. Furthermore, this discovery has shown that the structure of the whole universe, the planets, the stars, and all the organizing and administering intelligence [of Natural Law], are available in the structures and functions of the human physiology.
>
> Everyone is truly the embodiment of total Natural Law; everyone is truly cosmic. When we develop our full brain, our full potential, we rise to the ability to spontaneously think and act

in accordance with all the laws of nature because the laws of nature are lively within our consciousness and physiology.

Maharishi explains that the Vedic literature is a blueprint for how the creation is structured and how to avoid problems and human suffering. Just as a blueprint comes with the building to show how it has been constructed and how it should be maintained, the Vedic literature comes with the creation, as a timeless guide for how life should be maintained.

The Power of Coherent Consciousness in Maintaining Harmonious Life

In explaining the practical value of the strategies in the Vedic literature, Maharishi has restored the understanding that consciousness plays the key role in overcoming society's problems. Because of the interconnectedness of everyone at the deepest level of human consciousness, Maharishi Vedic Science℠ holds that the principal way to maintain harmonious life and overcome mass calamity is through strategies that promote coherence in the collective consciousness of the society.

If the collective consciousness in a city is settled and coherent, based on the sum total of the individuals in the city having a more settled and coherent consciousness, then the laws of nature in that city are not disturbed and these laws of nature will support human endeavors. On the other hand, if the collective consciousness in the city is agitated and stressed, the laws of nature are disturbed and diminished, resulting in widespread suffering.

To make the collective consciousness in any locale more peaceful and coherent, the Yogic Flyers and pandits will first practice their techniques of consciousness to settle their own minds and to generate the correct fluctuations in their state of consciousness and in the surroundings. This is crucial to the effectiveness of the Vedic defense technologies. Maharishi discovered that the practice of the ancient technique of Yogic Flying and the recitations by the pandits of the Vedic sounds gain effectiveness when these procedures are performed from the level of *Atma*, that perfectly silent and perfectly coherent transcendental field. This is the catalyst that makes the procedures maximally effective.

Transcendent experiences have been glowingly described in the literature of the East and West through the ages. Poets such as Wadsworth and Whitman, and philosophers like Emerson, Socrates, and Plato, as well as the ancient Vedic sages, describe the transcendent experience as a profound experience, and sometimes as a "religious" experience because of its transforming nature. Maharishi explains that the transcendental field, experienced when the mind transcends all thoughts, is the "home of all the laws of nature," and the seat of the almighty power of nature. Maharishi says this transcendent experience "awakens the divinity in man." He says:

> In order to use the almighty power of nature, one has to actually put oneself in the hands of the almighty power of nature.... If one is able to submit oneself to nature [by experiencing the transcendental field] then nature will react to his needs...because all the laws of nature are for the creation and evolution of all the beings and creatures of the entire cosmos.

Because of the peaceful and even blissful state that is experienced during the practice of the Transcendental Meditation technique, sometimes people question whether the technique is a form of prayer. The difference between Maharishi's program and individuals praying for peace, is that meditators and Yogic Flyers are not thinking about anything or wishing or asking for anything in particular. The purpose of Maharishi's Vedic defense strategies is to simply experience the perfect or near perfect *coherence* in consciousness that results from experiencing the transcendental field through the Vedic procedures. This automatically enlivens the transcendental field, and radiates a state of peace and coherence in the surroundings.

If the collective consciousness in a city is settled and coherent, based on the sum total of the individuals in the city having a more settled and coherent consciousness, then the laws of nature in that city are not disturbed and these laws of nature will support human endeavors.

The coherence in the individual and the coherence in collective consciousness is what allows the program to succeed. This experience of perfect coherence is vastly different from many people simply thinking a similar thought or from group prayer, in the same way that laser light, where the light waves are *perfectly coherent*, is vastly different from an ordinary light bulb where the light waves are not coherent. Less than a single watt in a laser beam cannot be looked at with the human eye because the light is so powerful. This is the power associated with coherent states throughout nature, and mathematically, with *perfect coherence*, physics tells us that the size of the group gets squared in terms of the influence that can be generated.

As mentioned in Chapter 1, if music from the same source is played through two loudspeakers placed next to one another, the sound waves from both speakers will be coherent, giving the two speakers the same volume of four speakers separately placed. This occurs due to the principle of *constructive interference* in physics. In the same way that perfectly coherent light waves produce a powerful laser beam, society becomes measurably stronger from the coherence of Maharishi's Vedic defense experts.

Scientists studying Maharishi's programs have found that the positive influence in society from people practicing the Transcendental Meditation and Yogic Flying programs dramatically increases if the people are all performing their techniques at the same time and from the same location. As previously explained, the effect is squared and 8,000 Yogic Flyers in close proximity have the influence of 64 million Yogic Flyers not in proximity. This is the remarkable power behind Maharishi's Vedic peace technologies. ■

FOUR

The Principles of Modern Science at the Basis of Maharishi's Vedic Defense

From the perspective of modern science, the benefits of the experience of the transcendental field have been well documented. The Transcendental Meditation technique was introduced to the United States by Maharishi in the early 1960s, and is the most thoroughly researched and most widely practiced meditation technique in the world, popularly valued for its ability to overcome stress.

Over 600 research studies conducted at more than 200 independent research institutions in 27 countries show the practical benefits. Because the mind and body function in an integrated manner, as the mind experiences its least excited state, the body also learns to function in a more relaxed and orderly fashion. The research shows that during a 20-minute session, the TM meditator experiences a markedly increased basal skin resistance (an indicator of deep relaxation)[1], oxygen consumption declines precipitously (much faster than during sleep),[2] blood lactate levels decrease significantly (high concentrations of lactate are associated with anxiety),[3] the hormone cortisol (found in large concentrations during stress) decreases,[4] serotonin increases (low serotonin is associated with aggression and violence),[5] and the EEG brain wave patterns become coherent.[6]

As a result of regularly practicing the Transcendental Meditation technique, meditators gain numerous practical benefits in all areas of life including marked improvements in physical and mental health, increased mental alertness and creativity, and more harmonious relationships with others.

Physiological Indicators of Deep Rest

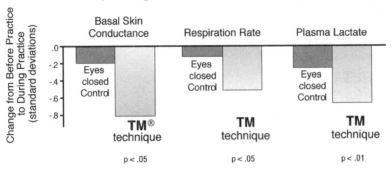

This chart shows the marked physiological changes during the practice of the TM technique. The research shows a level of rest more profound than deep sleep.

The Transcendental Meditation technique is practiced for two 20-minute sessions each day, in the morning and again in the late afternoon or early evening. The technique itself is effortless and involves no concentration or contemplation. The effort of concentration, as well as contemplative activity, are counterproductive since the goal of this technique is to achieve a least-active (least-excited) state of mind. Practicing the technique also does not require any change in lifestyle or diet. It requires no acceptance of any philosophical teaching and is not a religion. Rabbis, priests, Muslims, Hindus, Buddhists, and people from every religion practice the technique while at the same time adhering to their own religious faith. Moreover, the benefits of the Transcendental Meditation technique are not based on faith or even a belief that the benefits will come. The technique itself causes the mind *and* body to gain a least-excited and coherent state, whether the practitioner believes this will occur or not.

However, while most people learn the Transcendental Meditation technique for the benefits in overcoming stress, that is only a small part of why they continue to practice the technique over the years. It is the experience of the transcendent state, and the numerous benefits from the continuous and spontaneous development of higher states of consciousness, that cause meditators to continue in their practice.

The Value of Transcendent Experiences from the Perspective of Modern Science

From the perspective of modern science, as well as Maharishi's explanations of Vedic science, the *coherence* in consciousness resulting from the practice of Maharishi's programs underlies their success. *Coherence*, in general, means a high degree of orderliness, but it has a specific meaning when applied to the measurement of the electrical activity of the brain. The electrical activity of the brain is measured by attaching electrodes to the scalp of a subject and then amplifying this signal. The resulting measurement is called the electroencephalogram or EEG.

To determine coherence, researchers use computer programs that analyze the EEG or brain wave patterns. First the EEG pattern is examined in terms of the frequency of the brain waves, that is, the number of brain waves in a second. Slower waves usually are seen during sleep and faster waves during wakefulness. Next these waves can be measured in terms of their amplitude, that is, the peak height of the wave. For example, during the deepest stages of sleep there are high amplitude waves of about 2–4 cycles per second called delta waves, while during wakefulness there are low amplitude faster waves called beta waves.

In measuring EEG coherence, researchers must first specify a particular frequency they are interested in and then compare the phases of EEG waves between any two different areas of the brain. *Phase* indicates whether different waves are in step or synchrony with one another, that is, whether the crest of one wave coincides with the crest of another wave at a particular time. Coherence can range from 0, where there is no relationship between the phases of the EEG waves, to 1, where there is a perfectly stable relationship between any two areas of the brain. In a highly coherent state it is as if the two areas of the brain are in constant communication with one another.

Dr. Jean-Paul Banquet, a neurophysiologist, conducted his research on brain functioning while at Massachusetts General Hospital. He found that the Transcendental Meditation technique produced a unique orderliness in the functioning of the different hemispheres of the brain. He described it as an increased synchronicity in brain wave frequency, phase, and amplitude.[7]

Dr. Banquet's early findings were duplicated by Dr. Paul Levine at Maharishi European Research University, who used a mathematical technique to measure exceptionally high periods of EEG coherence.[8] His most common finding was an increased EEG coherence in alpha waves during and after the practice of the TM technique. The findings are presented in a vivid, computer-generated picture called a COSPAR (coherence spectral array). The charts below show peaks of strong coherence between two specific parts of the brain. For a peak to occur, the coherence must be above a value of .95 (remember that 1 is perfect coherence) for a period of several seconds.

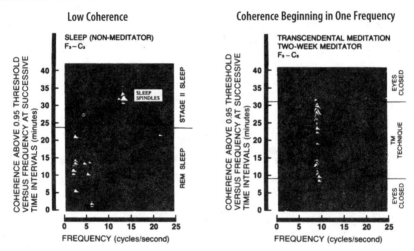

The charts above illustrate the relatively small coherence during sleep compared to the greater coherence during a 20-minute TM session by a beginning two-week meditator. While we think of sleep as being a very settled experience, the almost coma-like loss of consciousness during sleep is very different from the settled, yet alert, state experienced during the Transcendental Meditation technique.

For the meditator, the experiment begins at the bottom of the chart while the subject sits with eyes closed. After a few minutes, he begins to practice the TM technique. During the practice, coherence begins the moment the technique is commenced. The charts below compare a four-month meditator with the chart of a Yogic Flyer. These charts reflect the typical experience of the TM meditator. They show the growing coherence in consciousness as a person continues to meditate, especially in the Yogic Flying technique.

These initial studies by Dr. Levine showed the increased coherence in the brain, but did not determine how quickly the EEG coherence increased as a result of the continued practice of the TM technique. Later studies by Dr. Fred Travis and coresearchers in the EEG, Consciousness, and Cognition Laboratory at Maharishi University of Management in Iowa suggest that *individuals experience high levels of brain coherence during their Transcendental Meditation practice in only a matter of months.* Travis measured 22 people at baseline before learning the Transcendental Meditation technique, then again after 2, 6 and 12 months of TM practice. Travis' study shows that frontal EEG coherence increases to a high level after only 2 months of practice, and then remains at that high level when evaluated 6 and 12 months later.

Coherence Spreading to Two Frequencies **Maximum Coherence during Flying**

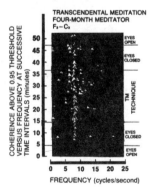
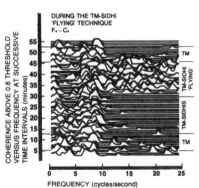

These findings show that individuals quickly master the Transcendental Meditation technique. This is unprecedented. Meditation, in general, is typically described as a difficult task at which only few can succeed. However, this is not the experience of those practicing the Transcendental Meditation technique. This technique is a natural, effortless practice, and it produces profound changes in brain functioning that are not seen in other meditation or relaxation programs.

Another important finding is that with the continued practice of the Transcendental Meditation technique, frontal EEG coherence occurs not only during the technique, but during a short eyes-closed period after finishing the TM technique, and also while performing simple tasks. This finding was also noted in the earlier study by Levine, and can be seen in the charts above. In the two-week meditator, the high level of frontal coherence occurs only after the subject begins the practice of the TM technique and then stops. However, in the four-month meditator we see a rise in frontal coherence before the TM practice, and it continues after the practice.

Optimization of Brain Functioning

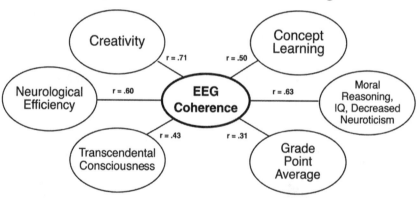

Higher levels of EEG coherence measured during the practice of the Transcendental Meditation technique are significantly correlated with increased fluency of verbal creativity; increased efficiency in learning new concepts; more principled moral reasoning, higher verbal IQ, and decreased neuroticism; higher academic achievement; clearer experiences of Transcendental Consciousness; and increased neurological efficiency, as measured by faster recovery of the paired H-reflex.

References: The chart above refers to data from the following three studies:

1. *International Journal of Neuroscience* 13 (1981): 211–217.
2. *International Journal of Neuroscience* 15 (1981): 151–157.
3. *Scientific Research on the Transcendental Meditation Program: Collected Papers, Volume 1*(1977): 208–212.

Travis and coresearchers also conducted a number of studies that show that significant brain wave changes in advanced TM meditators are seen outside of meditation, during normal daily activity. Dr. Lynne Mason and coresearchers have reported a similar finding for advanced TM meditators during sleep, in which the theta and alpha activity that occurs during the TM practice, is seen to occur along with the delta activity of sleep.

Collectively, these studies show that the twice daily practice of the Transcendental Meditation technique allows the brain to integrate the coherent activity experienced during the practice of the Transcendental Meditation technique. Coherent activity is increasingly found not only during the TM practice, but during the TM meditator's normal waking and sleeping states of consciousness. These are the first scientific studies that begin to objectively define the growth of higher states of consciousness, which has its physiological basis in this unique brain functioning.[9]

Yogic Flying

Maharishi's Yogic Flying is the most successful of the Vedic defense techniques for increasing coherence and thereby eliminating hostile tendencies, not just in the individuals practicing the technique, but in other individuals in the "vicinity." As previously stated, the vicinity here means the city, nation, or even the world, depending on the size of the Yogic Flying group. Maharishi derived his Yogic Flying technique from the *Yoga Sutras* of Patanjali, a great Vedic sage. Patanjali describes three stages of Yogic Flying. In the first stage, the body rises into the air in a series of short hops. In the second stage, the body is said to rise up and float or levitate in the air. In the third stage, Patanjali predicts passage through the air or actual flying (see Appendix A). While only the first of these three stages has been achieved to date by Maharishi's Yogic Flyers, what is important in the Vedic defense is not the outer results, but the coherent state of consciousness of the Yogic Flyers. The Yogic Flyers radiate coherence in the collective consciousness of those in the "vicinity," defusing violent tendencies.[10]

Yogic Flying students in Fairfield, Iowa

The Importance of Coherence to the Vedic Defense

When any physical system gains a perfect or near perfect state of coherence, the system itself undergoes a phase transition, resulting in that system gaining qualities that would previously be considered impossible. There is a marked difference between what may be considered ordinary coherence and the effects found throughout nature when a system, including the human physiology, gains a perfectly coherent state.

The *Third Law of Thermodynamics* in physics describes what happens when perfect coherence is gained. This law of nature states that when the temperature of any substance is lowered, the molecular activity of the substance becomes more orderly or coherent. Since temperature is just a technical term for activity, *the Third Law of Thermodynamics actually says that any physical system can become more orderly by settling or calming the system.* This is the principle behind the success of the Transcendental Meditation technique and Yogic Flying in eliciting a coherent state of consciousness and coherent brain wave activity. As the mind is allowed to become increasingly settled during meditation, increased orderliness necessarily results due to the Third Law of Thermodynamics. Moreover, this fundamental law of nature goes on to say that when a physical system is functioning from its maximally settled or least-excited state, that system will be perfectly orderly or perfectly coherent in its functioning.

The 2001 Nobel Prize in physics was given to three physicists who, using the principles of the Third Law of Thermodynamics, produced a new state of matter (Bose-Einstein condensate) by freezing (calming) the activity of several thousand small atoms, essentially eliminating their level of activity. This was accomplished by reducing the temperature of the system to nearly absolute zero, or minus 273 degrees centigrade. In this state the superatoms "sing in unison," according to MIT professor Wolfgang Ketterle, one of the winners of the Nobel Prize, giving scientists "unprecedented control over the fundamental building blocks of nature."

Similarly, Vedic science has long held that unprecedented control over the building blocks of nature is gained by experiencing *Atma,* a perfectly coherent state of consciousness. Something quite extraordinary happens when the mind crosses a certain threshold and has a transcendent experience as it becomes completely settled and coherent. As Maharishi explains, we gain the ability "to use the almighty power of nature." Again, Maharishi is speaking literally.

The Exceptional Characteristics of Coherent States in Nature

What are the exceptional qualities of perfectly coherent states?[11] Helium gas requires a temperature just 4.2 degrees above absolute zero to liquefy, and unlike most other liquids, it never freezes into a solid. However, something very dramatic happens to liquid helium as the temperature approaches absolute zero. The atoms in ordinary liquid helium exhibit random wave activity, but when the temperature is reduced to within 2° of absolute zero, all the atoms become aligned, producing a single coherent "quantum-mechanical wave." Helium is then said to be in a "superfluid" state. This is illustrated in the figure below.

Ordinary liquid helium is a bubbling, boiling fluid despite its relatively low temperature because its ability to conduct heat is so poor. Superfluid helium, however, doesn't bubble or boil—it is completely still because its ability to conduct heat suddenly increases a millionfold. Any heat is carried smoothly to the surface without disturbance. Something startling also happens to the viscosity of a superfluid. The viscosity or thickness of a fluid determines how easy it is to stir. Honey has a high viscosity, water a lower viscosity, and air still lower. Amazing, superfluid helium is frictionless and has a viscosity of zero. When stirred, it offers no resistance whatsoever. Its flexibility is such that if a fire hose were spraying superfluid helium at your finger under 1,000 pounds of pressure, it would go around the finger without any friction.

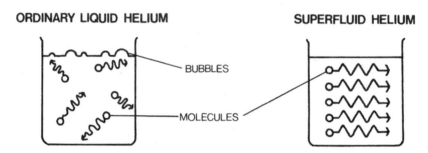

Superfluids are a fourth state of matter, uniquely different from the other three states: solid, liquid, and gaseous. The high degree of internal coherence in superfluids is the basis for their remarkable properties such as zero viscosity. Similarly, the state of transcendental consciousness achieved during the Transcendental Meditation technique is also a fourth state, in this case a fourth state of consciousness, different from waking, dreaming or sleeping states. Similar to superfluidity, the extraordinary properties of transcendental consciousness—for our purposes, the ability of consciousness to eliminate friction in the society—are also the natural consequences of the high degree of coherence present in this state.

Constructive Interference

Light is another example of how maximum coherence produces a uniquely powerful influence. Coherent light waves (lasers), for example, derive their power from a principle of nature known as *constructive interference.* Light, as well as all physical activity, including sound and the electrical activity of the brain, exhibit wavelike characteristics. If the peak of one wave falls directly on the peak of another, that is, if the frequency, phase, and amplitude are the same, the two waves multiply in power and the effect is squared. This is *constructive interference*. On the other hand, if the waves are not coherent, the peak of one falls on the base of the other, and they cancel each other out. This is *destructive interference*.

Constructive Interference

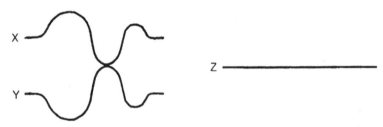

Wave A falling on Wave B, in the figure above, constructively produces Wave C having greater amplitude or power.

Destructive Interference

Wave X falling on Wave Y destructively produces Wave Z, which would result in silence in the case of sound, and darkness in the case of light.

Light is produced by the vibration of electrons. Because of the chaotic motion of heat in the filaments, the ordinary light bulb produces incoherent waves. Coherent light waves are produced by lasers. This light has waves that are all in the same direction, frequency, amplitude, and phase, resulting in the special properties of the laser beam. A laser light of one-half watt aimed at a piece of paper would cause it to burst into flame.

Stronger lasers shatter atoms and produce lightning flashes. Coherent laser light also brings out the interference patterns of a hologram allowing us to see in a new dimension. The power of consciousness, in its perfectly coherent state, is like the power of the laser beam and, again, is a natural consequence of perfect coherence.

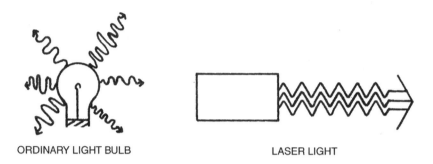

ORDINARY LIGHT BULB   LASER LIGHT

Superconductivity

One other example of how maximum coherence creates exceptional new properties is seen in the state of superconductivity. Superconductors also derive their exceptional properties by creating near perfect coherence through the use of ultra low temperature (low activity) compounds. A superconducting compound will conduct electricity without any resistance whatsoever (resistance is undesirable because it produces losses in the energy flowing through the material). Using these principles, researchers have developed a superconducting magnetic device that is capable of sensing change in a magnetic field as much as 100 billion times weaker than the force that moves the needle on a compass.

The perfect coherence of superconductivity is also able to create a phenomenon that is known as *magnetic-levitation,* permitting trains to "float" on strong superconducting magnets and virtually eliminating friction between the train and its tracks. Magnetic levitation, far from being theoretical, has been used effectively for years in Japan.

Magnetic levitation is derived from a highly coherent internal state that is analogous to the experience of thousands of individuals who have learned the Yogic Flying technique. Yogic Flying generates enough coherence to allow the body to "lift up," and in its more advanced stages is said to enable an individual to levitate.

Maharishi's Yogic Flying technique was described in ancient times by the Vedic sage, Patanjali. Though Patanjali described the technique of Yogic Flying, throughout history there have been relatively few people who could successfully achieve any of the stages of Yogic Flying (see Appendix A). Maharishi has explained that Patanjali's

> Something quite extraordinary happens when the mind crosses a certain threshold and has a transcendent experience as it becomes completely settled and coherent.

techniques work only on the basis of a coherent state of consciousness. The Yogic Flying technique only works when the technique is practiced in the coherent state of mind that is brought about through the Transcendental Meditation technique (a coherent state of mind, here, means coherent brain activity).

Nature's Defense Mechanisms

According to modern science, as the coherence of any physical system is increased, its ability to defend itself against disorder and outside influences is naturally enhanced. According to Maharishi's Vedic science, the same principle applies to consciousness. As the coherence in the collective consciousness of the society is increased, its ability to defend itself from disturbing influences is naturally increased. Maharishi's program to protect the nation from acts of mass destruction creates what is known in the Vedic literature as *Rastriya Kavatch*, an invincible armor of defense for the nation. Maharishi says this armor "prevents the birth of an enemy," meaning that it prevents an individual from gaining the status of an enemy.

While man has created smart bombs, sophisticated vaccines, and massive intelligence gathering networks, there is no man-made defense system or weapon that can effectively protect any nation or individual from terrorist acts of mass destruction. However, the bedrock of

Maharishi's Vedic defense is the recognition that there is a higher intelligence at work in nature's functioning. It is that intelligence, lively in every grain of creation, which can be seen naturally regulating everything from the human physiology to the movement of the planets with infinite precision. Maharishi calls that higher intelligence *Natural Law,* and the transcendental field is often referred to as the Unified Field of Natural Law. The practice of the Vedic peace technologies "stirs" the transcendental field, enlivening that higher intelligence in nature that underlies everyone and everything. When fully enlivened, this approach holds that Natural Law contains an *invincible aspect,* which can protect entire nations from harm.

Invincibility throughout Nature

From the deepest level of nature we can see very real examples of invincibility, for example, in the DNA. The internal structure of DNA has the property of being remarkably stable, with specialized self-repair mechanisms and enzymes that help maintain the invincibility of DNA's information. Some biologists actually view the entire purpose of an organism as nothing other than a means to preserve the DNA and to insure that its information is passed from one generation to the next. Through these and other mechanisms the DNA has been preserved and passed from one generation to the next for over four billion years.

Another example of the invincibility in our physiology is the immune system. This powerful defense system is able to recognize and destroy an enormous number and variety of foreign invaders. If a microorganism should penetrate our skin, the immune system has many ways of destroying it. In some cases the invader will first be targeted by antibodies, which are tiny chemicals that recognize and mark the invader for destruction. Once the invader is marked it attracts a number of cells, which, through their own form of biological and chemical warfare, eliminate any threat to the body.

The body also naturally defends itself from disrupting influences through regulatory mechanisms within the brain that enable the body to adapt to changes in the environment and maintain internal stability. One of the most important of these areas is the hypothalamus, which is a small group of cells in the brain regulating internal temperature, appetite (giving us signals as to when and how much to eat to maintain health), thirst (when to drink), water conservation, and the functioning of the cardio-vascular, respiratory, and endocrine systems.

The Hypothalamus and Its Regulatory Functions

A Small Coherent Group Upholds the Integrated Functioning of the Entire System

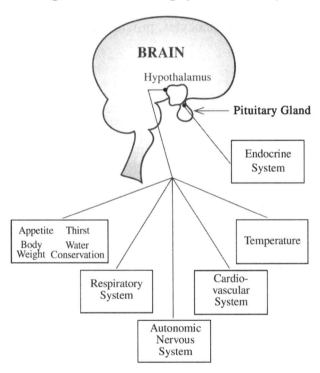

It is no coincidence that what we have come to recognize as the principal aspect in the invincibility of the body's defense systems is what can generally be described as the coherence or orderliness in the functioning of the physiology, often referred to as a state of balance or homeostasis. When the body becomes less than perfect in its functioning, it is due to some imbalance, disorder, or lack of coherence at the most fundamental levels of the physiology. Conversely, if we can maintain coherence or balance at these fundamental levels, for example, by insuring the proper functioning of the hypothalamus as the controller of many key aspects of human physiology, we maintain an almost invincible defense for the body as a whole.

Invincibility Inside and Outside: The Laws that Support Vedic Defense

According to modern science, as the coherence of any physical system is increased, its ability to defend itself against disorder and outside influences is naturally enhanced. According to Maharishi's Vedic science, the same principle applies to consciousness.

The same principles of invincibility that operate in the human physiology are found throughout nature: *Every natural system has an invincible aspect at its core.* In chemistry, for example, the nucleus and inner electronic shells of the atomic core are continuously found in a coherent state of least activity, which gives the atom its invincible nature, upholding permanency in the chemical properties of the atom. The outer electronic shells of the atom are subjected to ongoing change due to influences from surrounding atoms. When two or more atoms come together in a chemical reaction to form a molecule, the outer electronic shells undergo a dramatic transformation, while the atomic core remains completely unaffected and maintains its integrity.

One last principle of physics helps explain how the Vedic defense gains its effectiveness from the perfect coherence of thousands of Yogic Flyers. Unlike an ordinary electrical conductor, in which the disorderly electrons allow penetration by an external magnetic field, in a perfectly coherent conductor or superconductor, the coherent functioning of the electrons spontaneously prevents any external magnetic field from penetrating the superconductor's field. This phenomenon of invincibility, known as the Meissner Effect, says that the inner coherence and harmony of a system expel disturbing influences. The principle from both modern science and Vedic science is that *balance and coherence at the core of a system give it an invincible quality in the face of outside influences that would otherwise menace the system.*

Meissner Effect

An Example of Invicibility in the Quantum Physics of Superconductivity

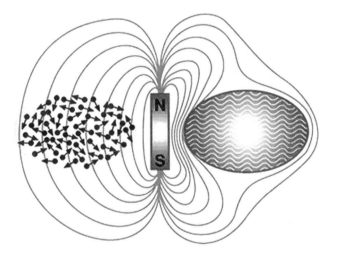

Ordinary Conductor	Superconductor
In an ordinary electric conductor, incoherent, disordered electrons allow penetration by an external magnetic field.	In a superconductor, coherent collective functioning of the electrons spontaneously excludes an external magnetic field, and maintains its impenetrable status.

Maharishi Effect

Scientists researching Maharishi's Yogic Flying program say that the Meissner Effect may explain how groups practicing Yogic Flying at the same time and in the same place are able to protect themselves, their city, and even their nations from hostile acts, sometimes referred to as the Maharishi Effect. This protection does not occur based on persuading criminals or terrorists not to attack, nor does it depend on debate, dialogue, or any intellectual or physical interaction with terrorists. It is just the natural and automatic result of creating a highly coherent collective consciousness within the entire population. The Vedic defense theory holds that a large enough group of highly coherent Yogic Flyers eliminates disturbing influences in the population as a whole. This is the principle; the next chapter describes the research results. ■

FIVE

Research on the Vedic Defense

"The claim can be plausibly made that the potential impact of this research [on Maharishi's Vedic defense program] exceeds that of any other ongoing social or psychological research program. The research has survived a broader array of statistical tests than most research in the field of conflict resolution. I think this work, and the theory that informs it, deserve the most serious consideration by academics and policy makers alike."

David Edwards, Ph.D.
Professor of Government at
the University of Texas at Austin

In 1977 researchers first reported surprising findings about crime in relation to the Transcendental Meditation program. In 11 cities where just 1% of the population had been instructed in the Transcendental Meditation technique by 1972, there was an average 16.5% decrease in the crime rate as compared to 11 control cities. In the cities where the meditators resided, an 8.2% average decrease in the crime rate was found from 1972 to 1973 in comparison to the previous five years (1967–1972). This finding contrasted sharply with an overall increase in crime of 8.3% from 1972 to 1973 in 11 control cities that were matched for geographic region, population, and crime rate, and with statistical controls for other demographic variables[1] (see illustration in Chapter 1). Researchers called this remarkable finding, that 1% of a population practicing the TM technique can reduce crime, the *Maharishi Effect* since the phenomenon had been predicted by Maharishi many years before.

Continued Research on the Maharishi Effect

In evaluating the initial research, the scientists wanted to know whether it could be proved that the TM meditators were the cause of the reduction in crime. Finding a correlation between two variables (the TM population and crime) doesn't necessarily mean that one caused the other. It could be that a third factor such as unemployment, or a change in the percentage of college students in the area, had caused the changes in both the TM numbers and crime. For example, a big increase in the student population might be the cause of more TM meditators and also be the cause of an increase in the number of law-abiding citizens.

A subsequent study by researchers at three universities (Southern Illinois University, West Virginia University, and Maharishi University of Management), therefore, sought to determine whether the increased number of individuals actively participating in the Transcendental Meditation program *caused* changes in the crime rate.[2] In this study, the researchers used a sophisticated statistical procedure to determine causation.

This procedure measured TM participation (the x variable) and the crime rate (the y variable) at two points in time. Researchers first compared the number of TM meditators in 1983 with crime in 1984, and then compared crime in 1983 with the number of TM meditators in 1984.

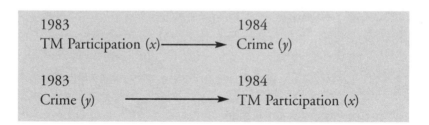

This method of analysis says that if a third variable (such as a change in the number of students in the area) is the real cause, the correlation of the TM participants with the crime rate would be equal no matter whether an increase in TM participants was found in 1983 or 1984. On the other hand, if the correlations are *unequal,* it strongly indicates that the relationship between the number of TM participants and the crime rate is not due to any unmeasured variable. Applying the strict statistical criteria involved in this procedure (known as cross-lagged panel correlation), the researchers found that the correlations were unequal, and since the crime decreases *followed* increases in the numbers practicing the TM program and not vice versa, it supported a finding of causation—that it was the Transcendental Meditation program that caused the decrease in crime. The percentage declines in crime were not as large as in the eleven-city study described above because of the smaller percentage of meditators (on average less than one-half of 1% in the various cities), but this study used a random sample of 160 U.S. cities, which comprised 25% of the total U.S. metropolitan population, providing substantial support for the findings.

> As predicted, scientific research shows that group practice of the Yogic Flying program produces a reduction in crime when just the square root of 1% of the population of an area participates in the Yogic Flying program.

Research on Yogic Flying

A second phase of research studies began in the late 1970s after Maharishi introduced the TM meditators to a more advanced set of Vedic technologies known as the TM-Sidhi program, which included Yogic Flying. Meditators who have been practicing the Transcendental Meditation technique for several months have the opportunity to learn this program. A period of time involved in practicing the TM technique is necessary because, through the TM technique, the mind arrives at the *experience* of the most settled and coherent state of mind, the level of transcendental consciousness or pure consciousness. The TM-Sidhi program, including Yogic Flying, then trains the mind to *function* from this transcendental level. It was theorized that the advanced Yogic Flying program, because it generates maximum coherence in the individuals practicing the technique, should produce an even more pronounced decrease in crime than the results seen for the Transcendental Meditation program alone.

As predicted, scientific research shows that group practice of the Yogic Flying program produces a reduction in crime when just the square root of 1% of the population of an area participates in the Yogic Flying program.

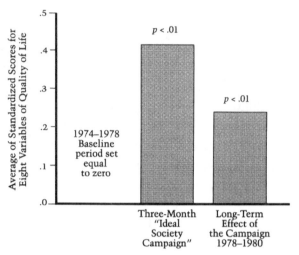

Improved Quality of Life in Rhode Island

A composite quality-of-life index significantly improved in Rhode Island during the Ideal Society Campaign in 1978, when a small proportion of the state's population practiced Maharishi's Transcendental Meditation and TM-Sidhi programs. Group practice of the programs was begun during the campaign and maintained by a smaller number in subsequent years, resulting in the long-term effect of the campaign.

One of the first tests of the Yogic Flying program in the United States occurred in Rhode Island during a three-month period from June to September 1978. Rhode Island has a population of about one million people, so it was predicted that some measurable reduction in crime and other expressions of stress could result when 100 or more people participated in the Yogic Flying program (100 is the square root of 1% of one million). The Rhode Island experiment tested this hypothesis with 300 Yogic Flying practitioners after the predictions were first published in the *Newport Daily News* on June 2, 1978. Using an index that measured eight variables, including crime, traffic accidents, mortality rates, and environmental pollution, researchers found a significant overall improvement in the quality of life in Rhode Island during the experimental period, as compared to a control state that was matched for geographic and demographic variables. The statistical analysis was at the $p = .01$ level, indicating 99% confidence in the findings.[3]

These early tests encouraged Maharishi to experiment further, and my [Dr. Wallace's] own involvement in explaining the Yogic Flying program began in 1978 just after the Rhode Island experiment. At that time, Maharishi asked me, along with several other scientists, to travel to Central America at the same time that 1,400 Yogic Flyers were sent to various trouble spots around the world, including Central America. These were demonstration projects to reduce hostilities in these troubled areas.

On my trip, I met with the presidents of Nicaragua and Costa Rica, the vice president of El Salvador, and top generals in the army of Guatemala, among others. It would be an understatement to say that not all of these individuals were champions of human rights. However, the Yogic Flying program is politically neutral, and our purpose was to persuade them to utilize Maharishi's programs to end the warfare that was devastating their countries. While we were in meetings with the heads of state explaining the science, Yogic Flyers from the United States and Europe were practicing their coherence-creating techniques in Central American hotels, and similar groups of advanced Yogic Flyers were doing the same in Iran and Southern Rhodesia (now Zimbabwe). In some instances the Yogic Flying was being practiced in hotel dining rooms, while outside the activities included Molotov cocktails, tanks, and machine gun fire, at least for a while.

Jon Levy of Ithaca, New York was part of the Yogic Flying group near Teheran, Iran. He said:

> Seeing the degree of chaos that prevailed [in Iran] made the task seem almost impossible. True, I had seen a profound transformation in my own life and in others I instructed in the TM technique but this was something else. When we arrived in Isfahan (a smaller city about 200 miles south of Tehran), we were welcomed by the sound of the hotel closest to ours being blown up and 12 of the city's banks being set aflame.

Tanks rumbled by our hotel as we settled into meditation and the TM-Sidhi program. As the first day turned into night, we began to sense a growing feeling of separateness from the turbulence going on around us. By the second day we were feeling very at ease, despite our external environment, and by the third day there was no denying the profound experience of "invincibility" which permeated everyone on the project. There was no fear or anxiety, only a strong undercurrent of silence and peace.

On the fourth day the value we had been experiencing over-flowed into our environment. It could be easily noticed, even by those not in any way connected with our project. The sun came out, children returned to their play in the streets, the troops were not so much in evidence, the shops reopened.... Peace prevailed throughout the land as our inner experiences became more profound. Nobody knew why. Almost nobody, anyway.

Perhaps the strongest single bit of evidence of our success occurred on "Army Day," an event which honors the national militia with parades and display of military hardware. It was thought opponents of the Shah would seize the opportunity with a bloody confrontation. Instead, the people threw flowers at the passing troops, and no shots were fired anywhere in Iran that day.

The peace project succeeded in calming tensions and reducing hostilities almost immediately, and the research that was subsequently published demonstrated the viability of the program. However, even before the research results were calculated, those of us who participated in the project remember the news accounts and other proclamations of *sudden change.* In Iran the tanks disappeared and schools and bazaars reopened. The BBC's Iranian correspondent reported the inexplicable calm in the atmosphere after weeks of fighting and chaos. In Rhodesia, war deaths fell from an average of 16 deaths per day to three starting in the week the Yogic Flyers arrived. Bishop Abel Muzorewa in Rhodesia, flanked by rebels who had turned in their weapons, told his audience that "peace has at last taken hold of our war-torn society."

Statistical data collected from the Center for International Development at the University of Maryland showed significant decreases in hostilities in the areas where the Yogic Flying took place during the 10-week World Peace Project that began in October 1978 (statistics that could not be accounted for by chance or by previous trends). A wave of peace had been created. After the project, we were optimistic that at least some government leaders would take advantage of the program. However, new paradigms are not quick to be embraced. *Our existing paradigm believes that war and terrorism can be defeated by threats, treaties, and military might. The new paradigm says that only a change in the collective consciousness will overcome war and terrorism.* When a critical mass of TM meditators and Yogic Flyers generates coherence in their own consciousness, the collective consciousness of the community (i.e., everyone's consciousness) receives an instantaneous influence of coherence, as demonstrated by the larger scale experiments that have now been conducted.

> The peace project succeeded in calming tensions and reducing hostilities almost immediately, and the research that was subsequently published demonstrated the viability of the program.

Larger Scale Experiments

After these relatively small demonstrations, major tests of the Yogic Flying phenomenon were undertaken in Massachusetts, Washington, D.C., and in Holland.

The Massachusetts Study

The first study on the effect of a large Yogic Flying group was in Amherst, Massachusetts, in the summer of 1979. The goal was to assemble enough Yogic Flying practitioners in order to affect negative trends in a more populous state and in the nation as a whole. Over a 40-day experimental period, a group that ranged from 1,570 to 2,770 participants gathered at the

University of Massachusetts. This was a number of participants in excess of the 1,530 participants that was necessary to constitute the square root of 1% of the approximately 234 million population of the United States at that time. There were two general hypotheses to be tested. First, that crime and other fatalities could be reduced in Massachusetts as well as in the nation, and that greater effects would be found in Massachusetts, as compared with other populous states in the nation, because of the proximity of the Yogic Flying group to that area.

Researchers measured the effects of the assembly on motor traffic fatalities, violent crimes, and eleven categories of fatal accidents, as well as on deaths from suicides, homicides, and undetermined causes. These categories were selected because public data on a monthly basis could be obtained for specific states as well as nationally. The study design compared the actual crimes and/or fatalities during the 40-day period of the assembly with the predicted level of crimes and fatalities for that period, both in Massachusetts and in the nation. The predicted levels in this experiment were based on the mean level of fatalities and violent crimes for the same six-week period of the year over all other years for which data was available. This included the prior years from 1973 to 1978, and the years following the experimental period from 1980 to 1981.

The results confirmed the hypotheses. In Massachusetts motor vehicle traffic fatalities were reduced 18.9% from the predicted level. For the nation as a whole, motor vehicle traffic fatalities were reduced 6.5% from the predicted level. Comparing Massachusetts during the 40-day assembly to all other states with populations over four million, the researchers found that in the other states, the mean reduction in traffic fatalities was 7.6%, predictably less than what occurred in Massachusetts where the participants were located. For violent crime, there were similar results. In Massachusetts the reduction was 10.1%. In the nation as a whole, the reduction during this period was 3.4% from the predicted level. The mean reduction for the other populous states was 2.6%, supporting the finding that something unique was happening in Massachusetts. The researchers also discovered that for each of the eleven categories of fatal accidents, and for the three categories of deaths from suicides, homicides, or undetermined causes, there was again a reduction from the predicted level, which ranged up to 26%.[4]

The Holland Study

The findings in Massachusetts were both confirmed and extended by researchers who examined the effects of large groups of Yogic Flyers in Holland. The large groups were enough, in fact, to influence the entire nation. The researchers looked at periods when there were significant decreases in crime over a ten-year period and found three such occasions. *All three times the decreases occurred when assemblies of people practicing the TM-Sidhi program in Holland exceeded the square root of one percent of the Dutch population.*[5]

Decreased Crime in Holland

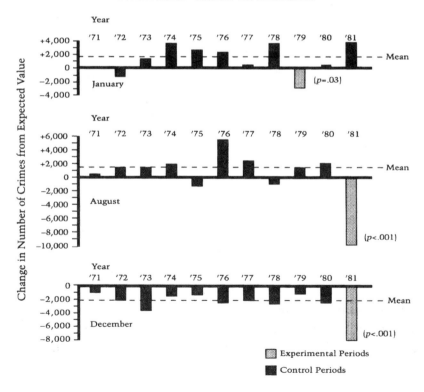

The Washington, D.C. Study

In 1993 one of the most important large group studies was conducted in Washington, D.C. Even before this study had begun, numerous studies had already been published on the group effects of Yogic Flying, and the statistics and methodologies of these studies were subjected to the intense scrutiny of peer review. For the Washington, D.C. study, physicist Dr. John Hagelin organized an independent board to advise on the study parameters, both at the outset of the study and as it was being conducted. The panel consisted of more than 20 sociologists and criminologists, representing a wide range of universities and institutions, as well as members of the D.C. government, police department, and civic leaders. The purpose of the Yogic Flying project was to reduce crime in Washington, D.C. since if good results could be achieved in the nation's capital, it was hoped that government leaders could not ignore the findings. The Washington, D.C. demonstration project was a highly publicized experiment, and the predictions of violent crime reduction were made publicly in advance. As with some of the previous studies, the research protocol specified a time series analysis of violent crime data (violent crime for these purposes was homicide, rape, and aggravated assault). Time series analysis and similar methods of making statistical predictions are frequently applied in the scientific community. The Federal Reserve Board, for one, places heavy reliance on time series models in economic forecasting and policy making.

> In the Washington, D.C. project, as the theory predicts, the over-20% decline in crime occurred during the two-week period when the group was largest, with lesser results when the group was smaller. Crime responded to the size of the group.

Decreased Crime in Washington, D.C.

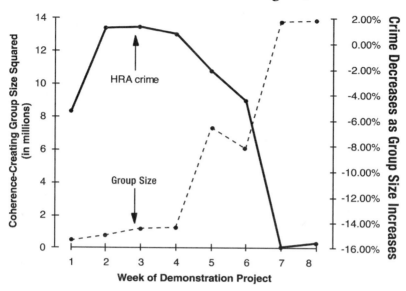

Time Series Analysis of Weekly HRA Crimes January through August 1993
Reference: *Social Indicators Research* 47: 153-201, 1999

Using time series analysis, the researchers developed a model of what the D.C. crime levels should have been during this period based on previous trends, as well as on the actual temperature, precipitation, and other factors that occurred during the experiment. These may seem like odd factors to take into account when analyzing violent crimes; however, it has been proven that levels of violent crime are significantly affected by temperature, precipitation, and occasionally other factors. For example, more violent crime occurs on the weekends, during heat waves, and when it does not rain.

Over the five-year period prior to the Yogic Flying assembly, violent crime levels in Washington, D.C. were found to be directly proportional to temperature. Even in 1993, just before the assembly occurred, violent crime could be accurately predicted from the historical data tracking both crime and temperature. As temperature increased, violent crime increased, and as temperature decreased, violent crime decreased. During the study, however, when the meditating group was approaching its maximum size, the violent crime curve dropped well below the temperature curve and stayed down for several weeks.

The D.C. Study Results

In the Washington, D.C. demonstration project, the group of Yogic Flyers ranged in size from about 1,000 at the beginning of the experiment in early June 1993, to over 4,000 for the last two weeks of the two-month project. Many of the participants came from all parts of the world at their own expense, spending their summer at several colleges and hotels in the area to demonstrate that this technology could work. Including financial contributions, the demonstration project cost over $5 million.

Yogic Flyers participating in the Washington, D.C. study

By the end of the two-month period, when the group of Yogic Flyers was the largest, there was approximately a 23% decrease in crime, a statistically significant number. The results indicated that the effects could not be attributed to temperature, rainfall, weekend effects, previous trends in the data, or police surveillance in certain districts. The analysis also predicted that there would have been a much larger long-term crime reduction of over 40% if the group of over 4,000 had been maintained in the District for 100 days. Increased coherence and reduced tensions begin almost immediately in the vicinity of a group of Yogic Flyers, and the effect builds over time.

In the Washington, D.C. project, as the theory predicts, the over-20% decline in crime occurred during the two-week period when the group was largest, with lesser results when the group was smaller. Crime responded to the size of the group. Nevertheless, the statistically significant decline in crime as the group size increased did not mean that there were not occasional anomalies. For example, in one week, when the Washington, D.C. group was relatively small, there were 10 homicides in a 36-hour period, which was significantly higher than usual. Looking at murders, alone, however, doesn't tell us very much because the absolute number of murders is so small (murders account for only about 3% of the violence).[6]

The Group Program and Collective Consciousness

It is important to note that the experience of practicing the TM technique in a group has nothing to do with any social or even physical interaction of the members of the group. The TM meditators in the group are all sitting with their eyes closed as they practice their technique, not communicating in any way with each other. The Yogic Flyers are silently involved in their own program. In fact, the multiplier effect from the group practice would be the same even if each of the meditators were in a separate room, as long as they were in proximity to one another and practicing their program in the same time frame. This is the common experience and research clearly shows that the effects are in direct proportion to the size of the group.

To those involved, the power of the group program in changing the collective consciousness is obvious. Hassan Sbaba, age 33, was raised in a religious Muslim home in Morocco. Today, he continues his religious observances, including prayers to Mecca five times per day. Hasssan came to the United States four years ago to study computer science at Maharishi University of Management in Fairfield, Iowa. He became interested in the University because he wanted to continue his education, and combine it with learning the Transcendental Meditation technique. After experiencing the peaceful collective consciousness in the University atmosphere, Hassan decided to remain at the University as a network engineer. Hassan said:

> The people in my country and those in America are not so very different, but there are big misunderstandings about Muslims. I was shocked when I came here to find that many Americans think that Muslims hate the American people. It is not true. Even with the conflicts that America had with many Muslim countries, the people distinguish between the positions the American government may take and the American people, who are generally well liked.
>
> Most Americans also think that in Muslim countries religion dominates more than in America, but even that is not true. We don't have Muslim radio and talk shows or anywhere near as much open religious activity in my country as in America. Americans and Moroccans have much more in common than they do differences, but most Americans with all the events going on right now, believe Muslims think differently than the rest of the world. It is difficult for the American and Islamic world to become integrated in a way that eliminates any tension if there is no attempt to understand each other.
>
> That is one reason why I think Maharishi's programs are so important. They are programs that anyone can enjoy, and they don't conflict with any religion. Here at the University we can also see what happens from the group meditation program. This campus is very different from other campuses. Here there are students from all different cultures and civilizations,

which may also be true at other universities, but there is a special bond here.

We all have the Transcendental Meditation program in common and the atmosphere is changed as a result of all the students meditating, which bring us all close and makes communication between cultures easy. There is an immediate respect for others in this environment. We are all on the same path. Even you [Jay] and I, due to our different backgrounds, would probably not be having this easiness in our conversation in another environment, or if we were not both meditators.

47 Studies

To date there have been 47 studies conducted on the Maharishi Effect. The results show powerful effects in significantly reducing violence in communities, states, nations, and worldwide.[7] The studies show reduced war casualties in various trouble spots in the world; reduced violent deaths from traffic fatalities, suicides and homicides in the U.S.; changes in what is known as the "misery index" in both the U.S. and Canada; as well as decreases in crime in New Delhi, Puerto Rico, the Phillipines, Australia, Merseyside in England, and in various cities in the U.S.

The studies, of course, do not show a complete elimination of violence and terrorism in the population affected by the Yogic Flyers, but Maharishi's goal is to accomplish that through the implementation of his programs on a large enough scale by assembling a critical mass of Vedic peace experts.

Maharishi Effect: Increased Orderliness

Decreased Urban Crime through Group Practice of the
Transcendental Meditation and Yogic Flying Programs

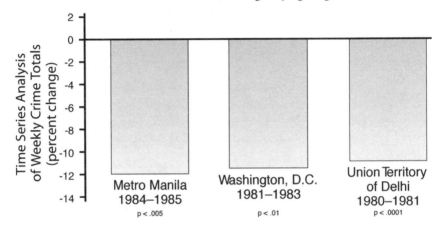

During periods when groups practicing the Transcendental Meditation and Yogic Flying programs exceeded the square root of one percent of the population, crime decreased in Metro Manila, Philippines (mid-August 1984 to late January 1985); Washington, D.C. (October 1981 to October 1983); and the Union Territory of Delhi, India (November 1980 to March 1981). Time series analysis verified that these decreases in crime could not have been due to trends or cycles of crime, or to changes in police policies and procedures.

References:
1. *The Journal of Mind and Behavior* 8 (1987): 67–104.
2. *The Journal of Mind and Behavior* 9 (1988): 457–486.

The Vedic literature considers mass destruction in any state or nation, whether from weapons or from epidemics of disease, to have a similar cause—mass violations of the laws of nature in that particular region. To overcome these problems the antidote from the Vedic literature is also similar and utilizes the Vedic preventive strategies. The critical factor in overcoming epidemics, according to modern science and Vedic science, is to generate in the population a critical mass of individuals who can counteract those who would otherwise infect others by spreading disease or terrorist inclinations throughout the society (see Chapter 6). ■

SIX

Treating Terrorism
as an Epidemic

"We must treat terrorism as if it were a chronic disease, always alert to the early symptoms and ready to employ, rapidly, a combination of treatments."

William S. Cohen, former Secretary of Defense

Because the laws of nature function in a parallel way at all levels of life, there are similarities between the Vedic approach in counteracting the epidemic of terrorism, and modern science's approach in counteracting epidemics of disease.

Terrorists, like germs, are ubiquitous, intent on destruction, and about as impossible to detect as germs until they do their damage. Moreover, any physician will say that, in dealing with an epidemic, it is impossible to kill all the germs. Similarly, the effort to kill the terrorists and those who harbor them must have the same lack of success. As in epidemics of disease, we don't ignore strategies like quarantines (in terrorism the comparable approach is restrictions on whom we allow to enter the country). However, the greatest success in dealing with any epidemic has been shown to come not from focusing entirely on the germs, but on hygienic and other prevention strategies that enliven natural defense mechanisms.

The Carrier Concept in Disease and Terrorism

Beginning in the late 1800s physicians studying epidemics showed that in the spread of disease, virulent bacteria were frequently carried by individuals who displayed no symptoms, or barely recognizable ones. With cholera and typhoid fever, for example, the German physician Robert Koch discovered that simply looking for active typhoid cases was not enough, and that only a

> The society then has a *collective consciousness* that is based on either the peaceful or the stressful functioning of its individual members.

bacteriological investigation could identify those who had been exposed to the infectious disease and could infect others. When eight cases of typhoid fever broke out in a German village, Koch undertook a systematic examination of all the family members and others who had contact with those eight who manifested symptoms. He found 72 people who were actually infected. They were *carriers* who could pass the disease to others. When the carriers were then treated, the epidemic was stopped.

Applying the carrier concept to terrorism, we know that many people who do not actually commit terrorist acts function as carriers. They are a support group for the violent offenders and their leaders. Carriers include those who preach hatred for others, or provide financial support to terrorist organizations, or who prey on the weak and the poor, enlisting martyrs to their cause. Conventional strategies should not be ignored in dealing with these carriers, but in the Vedic defense, the disease carriers are analogous to anyone in the community who is a carrier of incoherence and stress.

Maharishi's program of Vedic defense explains that everyone radiates an influence in the society that is either harmonious or negative, an influence that is either peaceful and coherent or agitated and stressful. The society then has a *collective consciousness* that is based on either the peaceful or the stressful functioning of its individual members. As individuals we influence the collective consciousness (causing it to be more coherent and harmonious or more negative and stressful) and we are also influenced by it. If the collective level of stress and agitation is high, an atmosphere is created that is conducive to violent acts, just as being surrounded by carriers of germs causes an increase in disease among those who are most at risk. As a result, the Vedic defense strategies aim to reduce the collective stress levels in the society.

The Concept of a Critical Mass

Continuing the epidemic model, some researchers have explained how epidemics are resolved by analogy to the physical concept of a critical mass. For example, we know that an atomic bomb requires a certain critical mass of radioactive material to trigger the explosion. Similarly, in epidemics of disease we know that when the number of persons who are carriers of an infectious microbe reaches a certain critical mass or density in a given area, it produces an explosive increase in the incidence of an introduced infection. If, on the other hand, you apply preventive health strategies and hygienic measures that enhance the body's defense mechanisms and strengthen the population's resistance to disease, then the incidence of disease starts to decline and continues to decline until no one or nearly no one gets the disease.

The theories concerning epidemics hold that an epidemic is stopped when a critical percentage of persons is resistant to the contagious microbe, since individuals are assumed to remain infectious for only a given time period. If, during that time period, those who have become infected come in contact with only a limited number of people who are at risk, over time the threat of the epidemic is eliminated.

For example, if a person carrying a weeklong flu comes into contact with 100 people during the week, one of whom gets the flu (a 1% infection rate), the virus passes through the community without any increase in the number of individuals with the flu at any one time (i.e., the original person who was infected no longer has the flu at the end of the week, but he infected one of the 100 people with whom he came into contact during the week, so the number with the flu remains the same). The flu epidemic is then said to be in a relative state of equilibrium. If, however, there is an increased concentration of persons with the flu or the flu bug becomes more contagious, and each person with the flu infects two people during the week, the equilibrium point is exceeded and the epidemic grows geometrically (each person with the flu passes the virus to two others the first week, who pass it the next week to four people and so on). Pretty soon we have a full-scale epidemic on our hands.

Terrorism, today, is spreading in much the same way as epidemics of disease. Terrorist recruitment and access to weapons of mass destruction can grow geometrically and may already have

> If the Yogic Flying group is permanent, this approach says that just as in epidemics of disease, the equilibrium point for terrorism recedes and ultimately reduces to virtually nothing.

exceeded the equilibrium point. When the infection rate doubles it results in every two terrorists spreading their agenda to four, who pass it on to eight others, and so on. The concern is that a critical mass of destruction-prone persons is being recruited and armed, which could tip the equilibrium, causing an explosive increase in violent attacks. In any epidemic when the infection rate is rapidly growing, the consequences of not taking effective action are highly predictable.

George Tenet, former director of the CIA, said the infection rate in terrorism is growing. Speaking before the Senate Intelligence Committee on February 24, 2004, he said:

> Al-Qaeda has become less centralized and therefore harder to trace, and it has begun to "infect" other individuals and groups with its radical and violent agenda. What we've learned continues to validate my deepest concern: that the enemy remains intent on obtaining and using catastrophic weapons.

The Vedic approach to defending against terrorism is to instruct enough people in the Transcendental Meditation and Yogic Flying programs in order to create a critical mass of individuals that provides protection to the society through the coherence generated by the group. Like anyone infected with a weeklong flu, if the terrorist, during the period he is at risk to commit an offense, is neutralized by a peaceful and coherent influence, he cannot infect the society with his misdeeds. If the Yogic Flying group is permanent, this approach says that just as in epidemics of disease, the equilibrium point for terrorism recedes and ultimately reduces to virtually nothing. This, then, holds out the hope for complete eradication of the risk of terrorism in the same way that epidemics of polio and smallpox have been eradicated. Maharishi's Vedic defense aims to establish a critical mass of 40,000 Vedic peace pandits in India, at least 8,000 expert Yogic Flyers in Iowa, and several hundred Yogic Flyers at peace palaces in the world's largest cities.

Internal Stability as the Basis for Outer Adaptability

The nineteenth-century French physiologist Claude Bernard (a founder of experimental medicine) said that environmental challenges and even germs only cause disorder or disease when the interior balancing mechanisms of the body cannot cope with the outside influence. Consistent with Dr. Bernard's findings, Maharishi would say that the seeds of violence and terrorism, like germs, are everywhere, but they only result in people committing terrorist acts when the internal balancing mechanism of the society, the coherence of the collective consciousness, cannot neutralize the external threat.

The way to prevent disease and disorder in the body is to insure that its defense mechanisms are functioning properly. If the internal stability or coherence in the body is lost, as, for example, if the flow of information from the DNA is disrupted, or if one of the regulatory mechanisms does not function properly, then disorder and disease will result. In the same manner, the Vedic perspective holds that if we create coherence and stability at the core level, that is, in the collective consciousness of the nation, the nation will automatically adapt to external circumstances and be protected from harmful influences such as terrorism. ■

SEVEN

The Terrorist Brain

"Bush, reinforce your security measures...the Islamic nation which sent you the New York and Washington brigades has taken the firm decision to send you successive brigades to sow death and aspire to paradise."

Ayman al-Zawahiri
Al-Qaeda second in command to Osama bin Laden
February 25, 2004

Is the brain of a terrorist any different from that of the typical man on the street? Former classmates and the family of Mohammed Atta were surprised that his final moments were spent helping to fly a jet airliner into the north tower of the World Trade Center on September 11, 2001. However, most of his friends had not seen the terrorist since he left Cairo in the early 1990s, and even in his student days the signs of disorder were apparent. During college at Cairo University, Atta was described as not very bright and a person with "no interests or activities." While he was not considered violent or hot-tempered, he was not tactful, and had poor social skills, and few friends. He was reported to be easily offended by perceived injustices, and if he did not like something, one college friend said he was "too frank and blunt with people. If he did not like something about someone, he would go up and say it to his face." A loner, Mohammed Atta was depicted in a caricature of his college class standing next to a military sign that said, "Coming Near or Taking Photos Prohibited," with a speech bubble that had him saying, "I don't hear, don't see, don't talk."[1]

Classmates reported that in college Atta had been strongly critical of Islamic extremism, but like many middle class Egyptians, he was also highly critical of Israel and its militancy. Atta came from a prosperous family and graduated from Cairo University with an engineering degree, then apparently was pressured to go to Hamburg, Germany, in 1992 for further studies. When he returned from Germany and bumped into a college friend on a Cairo street several years before the September 11 attacks, there were visible signs of stress, possibly the result of already having become associated with bin Laden's radical Islamic group. His friend reported that Atta was thin and weak and appeared quite unhappy and fed up with his life in Germany. His friend said that he had also seemed very bothered by the fact that he was not married. His emotional state was such that the friend said he felt very badly for Atta, who seemed quite sad.

While Atta showed many social inadequacies, if we had to rely only on his outward appearance and behavior prior to September 11, we would not consider him to be any more dangerous than thousands of other young men. Outwardly, Atta's inadequacies were not enough to suspect he would be the ringleader of the September 11 suicide bombers, and the one who, at least in part, conceived of the suicide attacks. *If we cannot rely on outward appearance or behavior to detect terrorists, is there any other way to identify those who are prone to commit these violent acts?*

Theories of What Causes Violent Behavior

There are hundreds of theories about what causes hatred and violent behavior, including economic theories that crime is caused by the unequal distribution of wealth and power. Certainly the refugee camps in certain Arab nations are a breeding ground for recruiting young terrorists because of the abject poverty and depressed conditions that make any alternative look good.

Sociological theory (social disorganization theory) links violence to disorderly or transient community characteristics. Disorganized regions, for example, have gangs and lots of violence. Pakistan is home to millions of Afghan refugees. According to Rashid Rehman, a journalist reporting in northeast Afghanistan in the late 1980s:

> If you have a war that lasts 10 years [the war with the Soviets], then you have children who were born in refugee camps. These children are raised with hatred as a daily diet.[2]

Rashid said he remembered a 13-year-old boy who waited eagerly for his 15th birthday, when he would receive ammunition for his AK-47, and he might have the chance to fight and gain honor for his family. Such hatred can readily be directed against Americans by those seeking to exploit these situations.

Another sociological theory (cultural deviance theory), holds that violent individuals have learned their values from deviant persons who reinforced the notion that violence is worthwhile. For example, in a terrorist cell, violent behavior and martyrdom are encouraged for a greater religious or cultural purpose.

These and other popular theories focus on how environmental or other external factors contribute to violence and terrorism. When we examine external conditions such as a large number of gangs or terrorist cells in the area, or whether the nation is disorganized and devoid of economic opportunities, and we try to determine whether those external situations will cause terrorist behavior, we get inconsistent information (i.e., some people will become terrorists and criminals and others will not). This is because external conditions "cause" violent behavior only if they have a sufficiently negative impact on the deeper, invisible levels of human life—on the functioning of consciousness and the parallel functioning of the brain and the nervous system, which are at the basis of our thinking and behavior.

The Proximate Cause of Violence and Terrorism

As discussed more fully in Jay's earlier book, *The Crime Vaccine* (Claitor's Books, Baton Rouge, 1997), virtually all theories about the causes of violent behavior can be tied together if we examine the stressed state of consciousness and physiology of violent individuals. If we focus on the internal effect of either our past actions or the external risk factors, this theory says, first, that there are thousands of reasons why people hate, some real and some imaginary. Gang members hate other gangs, inmates hate their guards, drug dealers hate those who would capture their turf, the disadvantaged may hate those who are prosperous, and terrorists hate people of a different race or religion, governments and cultures perceived to be evil, and so on. The point of focus, however, should be on how we can change the state of mind that is hateful, more than the reasons given for the hate, or on who hates whom.

The Vedic approach suggests there is an immediate condition, *a proximate causal factor*, that must be present for the individual to be hateful and engage in violent behavior or acts of mass destruction. That immediate or proximate cause is a stressed (incoherent) state of consciousness. In our judicial system, the concept of a proximate cause says that many causal factors may be involved in, for example, a car accident, but there is a proximate cause that must be present for liability to attach. If a car accident occurs at 10:00 A.M. on a crowded highway, the factors having a causal influence may include slippery road conditions, the failure of a road crew to sand the highway, and not having

> The final decision by the terrorist to cross over the line depends on the terrorist's state of mind at the time of the proposed attack, and this is where it must be stopped.

antilock brakes. However, the proximate cause is the driver's negligent manner in handling the car, given these external conditions. The negligence or lack of it depends on the driver's consciousness, his state of mind. Similarly, the terrorist act depends on the offender's state of mind or consciousness. Consciousness is the doorway through which the terrorist act must come.

Looked at in this way, the religious factors that may inspire al-Qaeda are really not so different from the hundreds of other factors that criminologists have identified in their theories of what causes violence and terrorist acts. To a criminologist the causes of terrorism include the unhealthy social conditions in Middle Eastern and other countries, disadvantaged youth growing up in refugee camps, the association with those who have terrorist tendencies, a lack of economic opportunity, cultures that condone terrorist acts, and the failure of the educational system. Unfortunately, using conventional strategies, there is *nothing* that can be done about any of these causal factors at least in the short run, and there are serious questions about whether anything can be done in the long term without changing the consciousness of those in these cultures.

The Vedic approach to determining the causes of violence is different from the approach of modern criminology. The Vedic approach asks whether, among all the causal influences, there is any single factor that is the necessary condition for the terrorist to detonate his device. Vedic science recognizes that there are actions in the past that may create a tendency toward violence, but the final decision by the terrorist to cross over the line depends on the terrorist's state of mind at the time of the proposed attack, and this is where it must be stopped.

The real issue is not why Islamic radicals and others hate us. People hate for many reasons, but if they can have such a deeply rooted hatred as to cause them to kill, it must come from a stressed and incoherent state of mind. The Vedic approach is different from what is commonly advocated for combating crime and violent behavior, in part because of a perspective that locates the inner cause of violent behavior in consciousness and directly addresses that state of mind.

The Terrorist's Brain and Nervous System

While our consciousness determines our behavior, consciousness cannot be seen in an effort to detect those with violent tendencies. However, a person's consciousness is based on the parallel functioning of the brain and nervous system, and there are distinct physiological signs that can help us detect those who are prone to violence.

The first wave of scientific exploration of the physiology of violent individuals began many years ago with the use of lie detectors or polygraphs. A polygraph measures the conductivity of the skin to a mild electrical current as the subject answers questions. In theory, we could ask the subject if he has terrorist associations. If he sweats over the question, the electrical conductivity of the skin declines, supposedly indicating untruthfulness. However, there have long been critics of the polygraph who say that the lie detector test measures a person's emotions more than truthfulness, and that guilty people can be trained to deceive the polygraph operator. Polygraphs have been controversial since their invention in the 1920s and are actually somewhat of an embarrassment in the scientific community. They are deemed inadmissible in court proceedings, and in 1988 Congress barred most lie detector tests from use in screening job applicants. The relatively poor experience with polygraphs may make scientists wary of using physiological measurements in this area or moving on them too quickly; however, significant research in the last 20 years shows a definite connection between violent tendencies and abnormal brain wave patterns, and altered levels of certain biochemicals in the body. The particular physiological characteristics of violent individuals also provide insights into why Maharishi's programs have been so successful in preventing violent acts and rehabilitating criminal offenders, helping them to become positive contributors to the society. The physiological changes from the practice of the Transcendental Meditation and Yogic Flying programs are in the opposite direction of the physiological characteristics found in violent offenders.

The Pinocchio Factor

In the story *Pinocchio,* we know when *Pinocchio* is not telling the truth because his nose gets longer. If all terrorists had such obvious symptoms, we would easily spot them. However, while terrorists cannot be identified using the naked eye, there is something of a *Pinocchio factor* enabling us to identify violent and immoral people using standard laboratory equipment.

Violent offenders and hateful people don't have long arms and a Neanderthal look, as was once thought, but they do show remarkable similarities when we examine their *inner* physiological characteristics. The principal characteristics appear to be low levels of serotonin (an important brain neurotransmitter involved in moods, and mental functioning), EEG brain wave abnormalities, inactive brain areas, and either low skin resistance (associated with anxiety and impulsive behavior) or a low responsiveness to stressful stimuli (accounting for the fearlessness of the psychopath and his attraction to the criminal lifestyle). While these common biological disorders have been identified in the past 15 to 20 years, criminologists have not paid serious attention to them because it has not been thought that these factors could be changed, and because not all of the factors are seen to be present in any one individual. A certain percentage of violent offenders may have low serotonin, but they do not show the other common physiological disorders, while other researchers have found abnormal brain waves, but not abnormal serotonin levels in the people, thus complicating the picture.

In many instances the research finding of one physiological characteristic, but not others, is just a function of how the research was conducted. Very few studies have measured more than one variable in any particular subject. Also, people react to stress differently (one person may get ulcers, while another gets high blood pressure), and in the same manner, violent offenders can have different abnormalities at the root of their violent acts. Nevertheless, because of the intimate connection between the mind and body, *some measurable physiological deviance will be present when there is deviant thinking and behavior.* This is important because when consciousness becomes more coherent through the Vedic technologies, the physiology normalizes itself and the physical basis of deviant thinking and behavior is removed.

Serotonin and Violence

How do Maharishi's Vedic technologies change the physical basis of deviant thinking and behavior? Research has consistently shown that *low* levels of serotonin are linked to aggression and violence. The Transcendental Meditation technique, then, should be especially interesting to those concerned about reducing anger and violence, since the TM practice has been found to naturally *increase* serotonin.

The first indication that violence was influenced by serotonin occurred in 1976 when the chief of neuroscience at a hospital in Stockholm found that patients with low levels of serotonin had a significantly greater risk of violent suicide. The findings were initially ridiculed, but in the late 1970s and early 1980s, researchers at the National Institutes of Health discovered that people who repeatedly committed violent criminal acts tended to have low serotonin.[3] Then in the late

1980s, it was discovered that the type of violence associated with low serotonin could be accurately defined as impulsive and hot-blooded.[4] Another
study of 58 prisoners convicted of manslaughter predicted with an 84%
degree of accuracy who would kill again after their release, based on their
serotonin levels.[5] By 1989, more than a dozen studies directly connected
abnormally low serotonin levels with aggression, including studies on
individuals with personality disorders, those with a history of alcoholism,
homicide offenders, arsonists, violent suicides, mentally retarded patients,
and males at a juvenile detention center.[6] The wide variety of violent
crimes committed by those with low serotonin indicates that terrorists are
different from others who are hateful and violent only in the particular
motivations behind their crimes. Whether a person kills while robbing a
bank, setting fire to a building, or making a political or religious state-
ment, the physiology underlying violence, and a callous disregard for life,
is the same.

To show that virtually anyone can become violent as a result of a
decrease in serotonin, researchers at McGill University in Montreal conducted a study using their own students. The first student to push a but-
ton when a light flashed punished his partner with a charge of electricity.
In the initial phases of the game, each student typically gave his opponent
mild charges that were no higher than he had received. But when the scientists had some of the students drink a concoction that lowered serotonin levels, the subjects began inflicting more pain on their partners,
despite receiving lower-level charges themselves. These students were then
given a large dose of tryptophan, which the brain uses to make serotonin.
As the serotonin increased, the amount of punishment they gave their
partners decreased.[7]

One caution has to be noted in looking at the serotonin experiments. Although many studies show a correlation between violent behavior and low levels of serotonin, in humans it is difficult to directly measure the serotonin levels in the brain, so the studies typically have to be
conducted on what is known as 5-HIAA, the major metabolic byproduct
of serotonin. These studies have measured 5-HIAA levels in the fluid that
bathes the brain or its rate of excretion in the urine. Some researchers have

questioned the accuracy of these indirect measures in predicting actual levels or function of serotonin in the brain, particularly since only 2% of the body's serotonin is in the brain. However, new

> Because of the intimate connection between the mind and body, some measurable physiological deviance will be present when there is deviant thinking and behavior.

research studies have found that low 5-HIAA is associated with a wide variety of criminal activities *and* with pronounced changes in mental functioning (likely caused by changes in brain chemistry), thus allaying much of the concern.

A Natural Means of Increasing the Offender's Serotonin

Research on the Transcendental Meditation program and serotonin was initially conducted by scientists at the Institute for Neurochemistry at a hospital in Vienna, Austria.[8] In 1976 they studied eleven healthy practitioners of the TM technique and compared their data with data from a control group of thirteen members of the clinical staff, chosen to approximate the age and sex distribution of the experimental group. The age of the TM practitioners ranged from 19 to 61 years and, on average, they had been meditating for more than two years. The researchers state that the selection of the meditators was essentially random. The results showed that the meditators had significantly higher urinary excretions of 5-HIAA than the control subjects, and that 5-HIAA excretion increased directly following the practice of TM, a further indication that the TM technique was responsible for the change. The higher 5-HIAA excretion was said to be "well above controls" and statistically significant at the $p = .01$ level, indicating odds of one in 100 that the results were due to chance.

To be sure that the Transcendental Meditation technique was responsible for the increased indications of serotonin activity, a later experiment collected urine samples from the subjects at three-hour intervals, twenty-four hours a day over several days. And in another study, six subjects were tested for 5-HIAA levels over a period of 89 consecutive days.[9] These studies also found a rise in the urinary excretion of 5-HIAA following the practice of the technique. Further studies on the ability of the Transcendental Meditation program to increase excretions of 5-HIAA were reported at the annual meeting of the Society for Neuroscience in Toronto in 1988, and at the International Journal of Psychophysiology meeting in Budapest in July 1990.

Reducing Cortisol (a Stress Hormone)

Dr. Kenneth Walton, a biochemist at Maharishi University of Management in Fairfield, Iowa, has conducted a number of studies on the effects of the TM technique on serotonin and cortisol. Cortisol is a hormone produced by the adrenal glands particularly in response to stress. It has, therefore, been called a stress hormone. Elevated cortisol levels have also been associated with certain types of aggressive behavior. Early studies on the Transcendental Meditation program conducted by Drs. Ron Jevning, Archie Wilson, and coresearchers at the University of California at Irvine, found reduced levels of cortisol during the practice of the TM technique, as compared to resting controls. More recent studies show that cortisol not only decreases during the Transcendental Meditation technique, but in meditators it is lower over long periods of time outside of meditation.[10] Dr. Walton points out that the effect of the Transcendental Meditation program on cortisol levels is remarkably similar to its effect on serotonin, except in the reverse direction—cortisol decreases while serotonin rises, both of which are beneficial.

Walton's studies show that when the physiology starts to function more normally through the deep rest of the Transcendental Meditation technique, the meditator experiences both low cortisol and increased serotonin, reflecting a less violent and more adaptive individual. Dr. Walton has pointed out what he considers to be the connection between cortisol and serotonin. Studies have shown that chronic stress results in chronically high cortisol. Numerous studies on animals also show that chronically high cortisol is actually responsible for chronically reduced serotonin; and that, conversely, reduced serotonin secretion prevents the body from stopping the secretion of cortisol into the bloodstream. Thus, according to Walton, "if the mechanisms in humans are the same as in animals, we are left with a vicious cycle that quickly gets out of hand as the elevated cortisol reduces serotonin, and the reduced serotonin leads to increased cortisol."

One other aspect of the changes in the body's production of cortisol is important to crime researchers. Researchers at Rockefeller University in New York first demonstrated that animals who were not stressed and were leaders in the group had low cortisol levels. Yet, when the animals in leadership roles experienced stress, their cortisol rose appropriately to meet the challenge. This is probably the most important finding to criminologists, and is similar to what Walton and his colleagues found in the meditators they studied.

In one study conducted by Dr. Walton and coresearchers, 29 males were examined who were randomly assigned to either an experimental group that learned the TM program or a control group that participated in a stress reduction class. Cortisol was measured in all the subjects before they learned the TM technique, and in the controls before they began the stress reduction class. Cortisol was measured again after four months in which the experimental group regularly practiced the TM technique and the control group had daily sessions spent analyzing stressful experiences and planning how to deal with them in the future. The TM group experienced significant decreases in resting cortisol

> Walton's studies show that when the physiology starts to function more normally through the deep rest of the Transcendental Meditation technique, the meditator experiences both low cortisol and increased serotonin, reflecting a less violent and more adaptive individual.

levels compared with the stress education group. Just as importantly, the TM group's cortisol levels rose higher than those of the controls during a stress response,[11] yet returned to lower resting when the stress was over.

The Physiology of the Psychopath

In the biological research on the causes of violent behavior, if you look at the cortisol research on violent criminals, what is perplexing is that a number of studies have shown that habitually violent offenders such as psychopaths actually have lower cortisol levels than nonviolent offenders or a less impulsive group.[12] However, their cortisol levels stay low and do not rise appropriately in what should be a fearful or challenging situation. These are the cold, calculating psychopaths, and this is likely to be the physiology of many terrorists.

The psychopathic personality was first described in the early nineteenth century as an individual who repeatedly involved himself in antisocial behavior. Psychopaths are also sometimes referred to as sociopaths, and one classic work described their major characteristics. They are generally intelligent with a superficial charm, relatively free of apparent anxiety or nervousness, and yet they may be habitually untruthful and immoral, lack remorse, have an incapacity for love, and are highly self-centered. *As might be expected of career terrorists, they often engage in continuous criminal activity, and typically have no fear of punishment.*

Physiological research conducted on psychopaths using skin resistance tests, hormone evaluations, and tests of EEG brain wave activity, has generally found that psychopaths have low arousal states. In other words, they tend to appear relaxed, with a physiological profile of high skin resistance, low cortisol, and slow brain wave activity.

This seemingly relaxed profile with a low cortisol finding (described as low arousal levels by criminologists) in psychopaths and certain other criminals shows how complicated this area can be. Since low cortisol is associated with relaxation and a lack of stress, this finding may seem odd. However, what distinguishes the psychopathic low arousal state (a probable characteristic of the career terrorist) from the physiology of the naturally relaxed individual, is that habitually violent individuals consistently show low arousal states along with low responses to stress. This is what is thought to cause their lack of fear and inhibition in committing crimes. They do not fear the consequences of their actions. Psychopaths are said to merely pantomime "feelings, but they don't have fears because they have so much difficulty feeling things emotionally."[13] As one writer said, psychopaths "hear the words, but not the music."

On the other hand, those practicing the Transcendental Meditation technique display a low cortisol state, but as Dr. Walton has found, their cortisol levels rise rapidly and appropriately in response to stress. This is a critical aspect of the cortisol finding that is in the opposite direction from the violence-prone physiology. Scientists are debating whether suicide bombers have psychopathic tendencies, or are just devoted to their cause, but certainly it would be easier to encourage a suicide mission in someone who experiences a total lack of feelings, resulting in fearlessness.

Improving Autonomic Functioning

Skin resistance is determined by what is known as the galvanic skin response (GSR) and is a very accurate measure of relaxation. Research on TM meditators shows that they have consistently high skin resistance (meaning that they are more relaxed). However, the ability of TM meditators to experience a deep state of relaxation and rest during meditation does not cause them to be unresponsive in activity. This was shown clearly in several studies measuring skin resistance and heart rate during stressful stimuli. In one study conducted by Dr. David Orme-Johnson, skin resistance was measured in a TM group and a control group after experiencing stressful stimuli. The meditators' initial response to the stressor (a loud tone) was at least as great as the non-meditating controls; however, the meditators adapted to the stressful stimuli more quickly than controls. Goleman showed TM meditators a movie of gruesome shop accidents. Compared with controls, the meditators' hearts started beating faster and their skin resistance responses were stronger, but then they relaxed and normalized more after each incident had passed.[14] This is in sharp contrast to what we know about criminal psychopaths. These individuals do not respond appropriately to what should be a stressful or fearful situation.

EEG Brain Wave Activity:
The Importance of Coherence

Brennan, Mednick, and Volavka, researchers who have long studied the physiology of antisocial persons, state that "a large number of studies…conclude that there is strong evidence for EEG abnormalities in criminal offenders, and especially violent offenders."[15] Some reviews, they point out, suggest that from 25% to 50% of violent individuals may have EEG abnormalities, whereas in "normal" populations the figure is 5% to 20%, based on clinical judgments of abnormalities rather than computer scoring.

In one study of 129 males, their criminal arrests by age 18 were predicted at age 12 based on their brain wave data alone. These findings were duplicated in a larger sample of 571 subjects in Sweden.[15]

If a person's brain is very disordered, he may be unable to care for himself and have to be hospitalized if his disorder is directed inwards, or he may be a threat to others if the disorder is directed outwards. The agitation and incoherence is the source of both disease and violent tendencies. Remarkably, if we can calm such a person's mind, he begins to gain control over his thoughts and activities. The individual's thinking becomes more orderly and creative when the mind becomes more settled. In a more settled state, depression recedes, and the individual begins to function with increasingly lower levels of dysfunction and unhappiness. In short, he becomes the average man on the street.

If we could continue the process of settling the mind, thereby making it more coherent and orderly (settling the mind and coherence necessarily go hand in hand), even greater results occur—a quantum reduction in stressed tendencies, and a quantum increase in the typical characteristics associated with human development: better health, greater inner satisfaction, empathy, and harmonious relations with others.

Changing the Terrorist Brain

The concept of stress was first identified as a specific syndrome in 1935 by the noted physician Hans Selye, a professor at the University of Montreal. Researchers everywhere now devote more than 1,000 articles per year to a discussion of stress and its effects. The syndrome that results in our becoming stressed was described by Dr. Selye as developing in three stages: the alarm reaction from the immediate event, the stage of resistance, and a stage of fatigue or exhaustion from the body's efforts to fight off the stress. In the initial alarm reaction, which is sometimes a *fight-or-flight* reaction, the body reacts to meet the stressor. Adrenaline is produced, hormones are released from the pituitary and other glands, and the individual adapts to the situation. During the second phase, Selye noted that some of the body's reactions persist until the stressful situation has abated. The expenditure of energy and resources may then lead to the third phase of excessive tiredness or fatigue. As a result of frequent stressful experiences, individuals may persist in the third stage as stress becomes a chronic condition that gradually destroys health and well-being.

Since Dr. Selye's early work, the stress response has been studied more extensively. Today, it is more accurate to say that a whole constellation of physiological changes takes place in the body as a result of stressful circumstances (not just the fight-or-flight reaction). A very high percentage of the population is affected by stress, and different people respond to stressors differently. For some, stress leads to anxiety or the inability to sleep, for others it can lead to ulcers or heart attacks, and for those with an extreme social, political, or religious mission, it can lead to violent behavior and terrorism. The underlying physiological changes may also be different—decreased serotonin, decreased autonomic stability, increased cortisol, irregular brain functioning, or all of the above. *But in every case, whether the person becomes ill or violent, there is a fundamental abnormality in the physiology, and both the mind and the body are affected.*

What is necessary is to take advantage of Maharishi's Vedic peace technologies to neutralize stress and prevent it from so disrupting the brain that it causes individuals to commit acts of violence and terrorism. This is accomplished on an individual level by teaching the Transcendental Meditation technique, and on a collective level by creating large groups involved in the Vedic peace technologies, especially the Transcendental Meditation technique, Yogic Flying, and the Maharishi Yagya® performances described in Chapter 10. These procedures eliminate the effects of stress in the individual and society by enlivening that higher intelligence that underlies everyone and everything. ■

EIGHT

Homegrown Terrorists: Preventing Them from Causing Mass Destruction

"Groups promoting extremist brands of Islam have gained a foothold in American prisons, and counterterrorism officials believe al-Qaeda are likely to try to use the prisons to radicalize and recruit inmates, according to a Justice Department investigation."

Eric Lichtblau "Report Warns of Infiltration by al-Qaeda in U.S. Prisons" The New York Times, *May 5, 2004*

In combating terrorism, there are threats from homegrown extremists, as well as from foreign nationals. We immediately think of Timothy McVeigh, who blew up the Murrah Federal Building, but there are many others. In July 1999, Benjamin Nathaniel Smith went on a three-day shooting rampage firing at 32 Jews, African-Americans, Chinese, and Koreans, all "tyrants," according to his World Church of the Creator. Also in 1999, Donald Beauregard, Brigadier General of the Southern States Alliance (SSA), was arrested for stealing explosives from National Guard Armories, revealing an elaborate plan for simultaneous attacks on power lines in the South and bombing the Crystal River nuclear plant north of Tampa (if he had succeeded in bombing the plant, Florida would have been uninhabitable until 2030). In 2003, Joseph Konopka, the 26-year-old leader of the "Realm of Chaos," and 62-year-old William Krar were sentenced to prison in separate incidents for possession of chemical weapons intended to be used for terrorist activity. The amount of chemical weapons they had stockpiled was more than has been found in Iraq.

Domestic terrorism is conceived by fanatics whose plans include everything from attacks on minority groups to elaborate plans to cause mass destruction and overthrow the U.S. government. The purpose of domestic terrorism is the same as foreign terrorism—to intimidate or coerce the government or the civilian population in furtherance of political, religious, or social objectives.

Domestic terrorism has been defined by the FBI as the use of violence by a group or individual operating entirely within the United States without foreign direction. According to a 1999 special FBI report on terrorism,[1] from 1980 to 1999 there were 327 successful terrorist attacks in the United States, including attacks on abortion clinics, assassinations, and attacks by extremist environmental and animal rights groups. A further 130 attacks were known to be prevented. In the 1980s, only 23 people were killed in the U.S. and 105 were injured by terrorist acts. In 1995, however, our concerns about domestic terrorism were magnified by the bombing of the Murrah Federal Building in Oklahoma City, which resulted in 168 deaths.

The distinctions between domestic and foreign terrorism lose significance as the evidence grows that extremist groups in the U.S. and elsewhere are establishing significant ties with radical Muslim organizations. A recent study by the Southern Poverty Law Center indicates that white supremacists, neo-Nazis, and Black Muslim factions are stepping up their efforts to seek alliances with foreign terrorists who share a hatred for Israel and the United States. The Chechen massacre in September 2004 at the Beslan school in Russia was masterminded by Shamel Basayev, a Chechen warlord who recognized that funds were available from wealthy radical Islamists and aligned himself with these funding sources. Basayev, not previously a religious person, took an Arab name, Abdullah Shamel Abu Iris. Then he declared himself the leader of the Garden for the Righteous Islamic Brigade of Martyrs and sent videotapes into the Arab world promoting his allegiance to the radical Islamic *jihad*. He obtained the funds he needed.

Unfortunately, local groups are natural allies with foreign terrorists. American terrorists, for example, have the ability to avoid U.S. security measures targeted at Middle East nationals, and foreign Muslim radicals have what the local groups lack—the resources for large-scale operations.

Mark Potok, who edits the quarterly intelligence report of the Southern Poverty Law Center, says that the neo-Nazi and American supremacists applauded the September 11 attacks. Unfortunately, it may have inspired them to think in terms of bigger and more destructive attacks. Neutralizing domestic terrorists, if we can do it, would eliminate alliances that could otherwise prove deadly in the future.

Terrorists Passing through Our Prisons

Approximately 99% of everyone who enters prison will be released at some time, either on parole or at the end of his or her sentence. Most released prisoners engage in repetitive violent crimes, spreading their personal brand of terrorism throughout the society. Some, at least, will be tempted in the direction of causing mass destruction. Based on dismal recidivism statistics, thousands of extremists will not be rehabilitated while passing through our prisons and will inevitably have further opportunities to cause destruction upon their release.

The most recent national study of recidivism in the U.S. was conducted in 1989 and showed that within the first year of release, ex-prisoners committed 29,081 violent crimes per 100,000 released prisoners, as compared with 539 violent crimes per 100,000 in the general population in the same year.[2] Released prisoners, therefore, commit approximately 50 times more violent crimes in the first year of their release than average citizens do in a year. They also probably represent the most highly stressed individuals in the society. Trying to rehabilitate them also makes sense because of the extreme levels of stress they contribute to the collective consciousness.

Does Anything Work in Rehabilitation?

At one session during an annual meeting of the Academy of Criminal Justice Sciences in Boston five years ago, Professor Kevin Ryan, then of Norwich University in Vermont, presented a paper describing the illusion of change in prisons. Ryan distinguished between real change and "pseudo" change, the latter involving a mere verbal pronouncement of change in which individuals pretend to have changed because they stand to benefit. Ryan pointed out that a mask of change is often donned by prisoners simply for the thrill of "running a con" on some gullible person.

Near the end of his talk, Professor Ryan was asked if he was aware of any program that had been found to produce real change in an inmate's state of mind, what Ryan calls a "veridical" conversion, as opposed to a mere "narrative" conversion. Professor Ryan said that his review of the literature took note of two programs that at least emphasized inner change: Alcoholics Anonymous and the Transcendental Meditation program. His report states that "despite the almost universal belief that Twelve Step [Alcoholics Anonymous] programs are effective, extraordinarily little research has been done to evaluate the effectiveness of such programs." Citing a 1989 summary of the AA research, Professor Ryan stated in his paper that "not one study has ever found AA or its derivatives to be superior to any other approach, or even to be better than not receiving any help at all...."

> Professor Ryan reported that despite the positive results of these research studies, the Vedic approach is ignored—the typical fate of new knowledge.

In contrast, Professor Ryan noted that the TM program had been well researched. It had been taught to approximately 2,700 inmates and more than 250 correctional officers in 28 facilities in the United States, yet Ryan reported that despite the positive results of these research studies, the "standard reviews of effectiveness research fail to mention TM." In other words, the Vedic approach is ignored—the typical fate of new knowledge despite the promise it offers for effective rehabilitation.

The Problem with Recidivism: The Cart before the Horse

The problem with conventional rehabilitation efforts is that they do not effectively deal with an offender's abnormal physiology (stress) and the incoherence in his consciousness. Prisoners themselves are painfully aware of the stress and tension in their lives, and any reduction in stress is much sought after. An inmate at the Augusta Correctional Center in Georgia, Butch Evans, writes articles on health for the prison newspaper. In one article he states:

> Stress. A daily part of our lives.... Stress is especially high for us due to our environment, concerns for the family's health and finances, our loved ones, will they wait for me, be there for me when I get out, and when am I getting out? This high level of stress will follow us into freedom as well.... How we manage stress, control it (and it can be done effectively) will make all the difference in our quality of life, now and in the future.[3]

Current approaches seek to reeducate an offender before they treat the underlying stress that makes him either uninterested in education or incapable of being educated. Yet virtually every psychologist knows that when you decrease tension and anxiety, the individual begins to think more clearly, concentrates better, and often begins to succeed where previously he experienced only failure. In addition, prison programs that have used relaxation procedures use relatively ineffective techniques developed by modern health practitioners who may have good intentions, but do not appreciate the subtleties of meditation.

The *TM* Program and Violent Offenders

In 1971, Pat Corum was the first inmate to learn the Transcendental Meditation technique in the California prison system. He was then serving two life sentences at Folsom State Prison, one of the most repressive, stressful prisons in the California correctional system.[4] After Corum, other Folsom inmates learned to meditate in what proved to be one of the most rewarding experiments in U.S. correctional history. On being asked by a reporter whether the use of this technique had changed things at the prison, Corum said:

> Inside at Folsom, numerous murders have been stopped. It's because the people no longer feel the inside tension, the hostility within, and the need to strike out. These men are just mellowed out. They're calm. They're thinking for the first time in their lives. And you get a man that thinks, he is not going to be in trouble.

It may seem like an exaggeration to say that numerous murders were prevented by the Transcendental Meditation program, but others felt the same way about how Folsom was changed. Ernest Merriweather also learned to meditate at Folsom shortly after the TM program was introduced. He said:

> We had some of the toughest groups, or gangs I guess you could call them, in the world at Folsom Prison. There was the Aryan Brotherhood, the Black Gorilla Family, the Mexican Mafia and others.... They were bent on destroying themselves and everything else around them.... Prior to [the Transcendental Meditation program] coming to Folsom Prison, if you looked at some of these people the wrong way, you were dead the next morning, or if you talked to someone the wrong way, you were dead, or if you borrowed a pack of cigarettes from someone and didn't give it back, you were dead. And [the TM program] brought us all together.... It really was a miracle to see some of these tough groups getting together in the same room and embracing one another.... It's still hard to conceive, but it happened.

The research on the Transcendental Meditation program at Folsom in the 1970s verified the effects described by these men. In their studies, researchers used what is known as random assignment cross-validation designs. Using this methodology, the same study is conducted twice on two independent samples, which are randomly assigned to different groups in an attempt to substantiate the results. In a study involving 115 inmates, researchers found that the Transcendental Meditation program significantly reduced anxiety and neuroticism. The first group showed reduced negativity and suspicion, and the second group showed reduced irritability, negativity, verbal hostility, and assaults.[5]

Inmates practicing the TM technique at Folsom prison

Hoyt S. Chambles, the supervisor of the Correctional Education Programs at Folsom, observed the effects of the program conducted at Folsom and described the reduced hostilities. He said:

> The small group of inmates who are now receiving Transcendental Meditation instruction appear to have better control over their emotions and lives within a very few weeks. I have personally observed two situations that would have led to physical confrontation before having TM instruction. However, these two different inmates not only controlled themselves but also received apologies from the other inmates involved after a cooling-off period.... Of other inmates that I have knowledge of before and after the TM instruction, there is a calmness and ability to discuss and talk a problem out

rather than using physical means to achieve their goals. My observations of the inmates taking TM instruction showed there has been a measurable accomplishment, that these men are willing to meet life head-on, but without any physical or violent confrontation.

Reports such as these led other prisons (including the Federal Correctional Institution in Milan, Michigan,[6] and the minimum security prison at Walpole, Massachusetts) to provide Transcendental Meditation programs for some of their inmates, and controlled studies showed reduced aggression and increased self-esteem, emotional stability, and maturity.[7]

Decreased Hostility in Prisoners

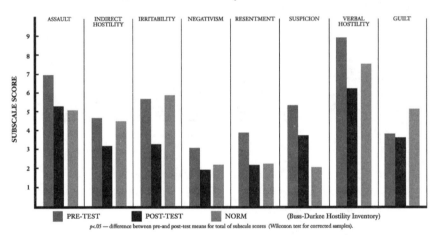

Reduced Anxiety and Increased Interest in Education

Numerous studies have also looked at the effects of the Transcendental Meditation program on anxiety in prisoners. One study was conducted in the 1970s at Stillwater in Minnesota and another was conducted at the Federal Correctional Institute in Lompoc. Each of these studies involved 30 inmates in the TM group. At Stillwater, the inmates were randomly assigned to a Transcendental Meditation group or a control group that was not taught the Transcendental Meditation technique until after the experimental period. Another control group consisted of sixteen inmates who did not want to learn the Transcendental Meditation program. Anxiety decreased significantly in the TM group compared with the control groups (at the p = .001 level, indicating odds of one in 1,000 that the results could have been due to chance). The Stillwater meditators shifted from being one of the most anxious populations in the prison to being one of the least anxious.[8] Similar results were found in the Lompoc study.

Immediate and Lasting Improvement

In other prison programs from 1982 through 1984, more than 700 inmates and correctional staff learned to practice the Transcendental Meditation technique in programs at several institutions in the Vermont Department of Corrections. The inmates also participated in related educational programs to gain an understanding of the positive changes they were experiencing. Several studies emerged.[9]

In one study, 129 inmates were pre-tested and subsequently post-tested up to fourteen months following instruction in the TM technique. This longitudinal study showed continued improvement in sleep disturbances, paranoid anxiety, anger control, and hostility.

This process of continuing change with continued meditation contrasts sharply with results of conventional programs. With most self-improvement programs, results decline over time. Initially, inmates may be inspired and motivated to behave better, but pep talks and purely psychological approaches often fail to produce lasting results. In contrast, the deep inner changes in mind and body from the regular practice of the Transcendental Meditation program have a lasting effect on the individual, which is the prerequisite for lower recidivism rates and public safety.

Dramatically Reducing Recidivism

Catherine Bleick and Allan Abrams conducted recidivism research on 259 male parolees of the California Department of Corrections who had learned the Transcendental Meditation technique, and their findings were published in the *Journal of Criminal Justice* in 1987.[10] They found that in comparison to matched controls, the Transcendental Meditation group had consistently more favorable recidivism outcomes every year, from one to six years after parole. Controlling for twenty-eight social and criminal history variables in what is known as "stepwise multiple regression," the Transcendental Meditation program significantly (p = .001, indicating odds of one in 1000 that the results were due to chance) reduced recidivism, at one year and up to six years after parole, while prisoner education, vocational training, and psychotherapy were not able to consistently reduce recidivism.

The researchers found that the men who were paroled within five months after TM instruction tended to have a worse recidivism profile than those who were paroled later and, therefore, had more time to practice the technique. This was one indication that the Transcendental Meditation program was responsible for the change. In addition, the average recidivism rate was significantly lower for the meditator group every year after release as compared to controls. Recidivism will naturally increase over time (for example, more people will have been returned to prison four years after their initial release, compared with three years). But as both the Transcendental Meditation group and the control group increased in recidivism over the years, the groups did not converge, and the TM meditators consistently stayed out of trouble compared with the controls.

Dr. Charles Alexander and his coresearchers at Harvard came to similar conclusions about this program's ability to reduce recidivism in a carefully controlled study at the minimum security prison at Walpole in Massachusetts.[11] Dr. Alexander's study followed the released inmates for more than three years and used not only a random sample of inmates as a comparison group, but also four different treatment groups: those in drug rehabilitation, a counseling group, and inmates involved in two self-improvement programs. The 53 prisoners who learned the Transcendental Meditation technique showed consistently lower recidivism rates when compared to the random sample controls and those in treatment.

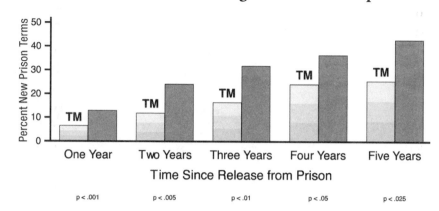

Reduced Recidivism through the *TM* Technique

How much better in terms of recidivism was the Transcendental Meditation group compared with the control group in these studies? Unlike conventional education programs, where the Bureau of Prisons is excited about a 4.2% difference in recidivism, the Bleick and Abrams study with the Transcendental Meditation program found that the difference was 35% to 45%. In the Alexander study, when controlling for the time of release (to avoid the potential bias caused by groups with later dates of release having less time to recidivate), after thirty-six months the Transcendental Meditation recidivism rate was 48% lower than the entire group involved in other treatment programs.

International Rehabilitation Programs

When Maharishi's Vedic approach has been introduced in other countries in prisons, or to correctional or police personnel, the results have been even more dramatic. This is because many of the programs in foreign countries have been much larger, involving thousands of individuals meditating as a group, and, as discussed earlier, those who practice the Transcendental Meditation technique in groups tend to have more settled experiences in meditation in direct proportion to the size of the group. In addition, these larger programs, of necessity, have had the support not just of the staff, but usually of government officials who supervise the activity of the prison directors.

In 1987, this approach was used by two prisons in the West African nation of Senegal. The director of the Camp Penal Prison in Dakar, Ilbrahima Sy, said that the penology experts in Senegal had long been searching for an effective rehabilitation program. His country's efforts had been modeled earlier on those of the Western nations. In a search for genuine rehabilitation, his administration attempted to institute the

> Successful TM prison programs involving more than 30,000 inmates have been conducted in Senegal, Sri Lanka, India, Kenya, Chile, Spain, Paraguay, Mexico, Korea, and elsewhere.

so-called progressive or enlightened reforms used in the West, since repressive measures, he said, "turned out to be a fiasco everywhere, even in countries referred to as the most civilized."

When the experts decided that only through work and the teaching of trades could a prisoner rediscover his value and become rehabilitated, some Senegal prisons, Mr. Sy said, offered farming, carpentry, masonry, automobile repair, and other workshops for the training of inmates. As in the U.S., the goal was to teach the prisoner a trade so that he could continue it after release and earn a decent living. However, Mr. Sy said the experience showed that inmates in the work programs who were thought to be well rehabilitated constitute the biggest number of recidivists. Once the Transcendental Meditation program was tried, however, Mr. Sy's inmate population changed dramatically for the better, and he felt he had finally found the key to rehabilitation.

The positive results convinced Mr. Sy and the director of the Senegal penitentiary system that the Transcendental Meditation program should be brought to the remaining prisons. As a result, except for a few prisons in outlying areas, the program was introduced in all Senegalese prisons. Approximately 11,000 inmates and 900 correctional officers and administrators were instructed in the Transcendental Meditation technique, and in yoga exercises, and received related classroom instruction in a program that took about two hours a day.

Two years after the program was introduced, Colonel Mamadou

Diop, then director of the penitentiary administration of Senegal, wrote a letter describing the overall results: an immediate improvement in the inmates' sleep, a sharp reduction in irritability and aggressiveness, greater confidence among the inmates, improved relationships between inmates, a marked decrease in drug consumption, and an almost complete cessation of fights between inmates.

Colonel Diop said that before the program was instituted Senegal prisons had an especially high recidivism rate since "there is no structure or scheme for the reintegration of inmates into society, nor is there any provision for work or jobs for those released." As a result, he estimated that in Senegal usually about 90% of inmates released after serving their sentence returned to prison within *one month.*

Inmates meditating in Senegal

Every year in Senegal there is a yearly presidential pardon for some of the inmates. *Six months* after the June 1988 amnesty, in which 2,390 inmates were released, there were less than 200 recidivists, and 80% of those consisted of the group that had not participated in the meditation program because their prisons were in such remote regions of the country. In other words, only about 40 of those who participated in the TM program returned to prison. This allowed the country to close three prisons for lack of inmates, and in other prisons there were sharp reductions in the number of prisoners.

After this experience, the Senegal prison directors were no longer skeptical that prisoners could be rehabilitated. In fact, thirty prison directors signed a proclamation asking, among other things, that words like "penal" or "penitentiary" and even "prison" be discontinued and replaced by expressions referring to the "reeducation" and "rehabilitation" that had become possible.

Successful TM prison programs involving more than 30,000 inmates have been conducted in Senegal, Sri Lanka, India, Kenya, Chile, Spain, Paraguay, Mexico, Korea, and elsewhere. In Brazil, the program was taught on a large scale at the police academies. In 1987 and 1988, 26,000 Brazilian military police learned the Transcendental Meditation technique. A number of studies were conducted showing decreases of 31% to 65% in disciplinary measures taken against the police as compared with the pre-TM experience, and a highly significant improvement in community relations as measured by a more than tenfold increase in positive reports from the citizens of Salvador. Other results included sharp reductions in tension, a significant decrease in physician visits, and greatly improved relationships with others.

The Enlightened Sentencing Project in St. Louis

In 1996 Judge David Mason of the 22nd Circuit Court of Missouri began investigating the use of the Transcendental Meditation program in a probation setting as an alternative to prison. His investigation led him first to a "softball approach," sentencing several offenders who had minor drug problems to learn the Transcendental Meditation technique. Excellent results led him to begin using the Transcendental Meditation technique with more high-risk cases, and again he was delighted with the findings. Over 100 offenders [their offenses included the use and sale of drugs, robbery, assault, child abuse, and even one murder after incarceration] have now participated in the program begun by Judge Mason.

In St. Louis, if a judge determines that an offender should be placed on probation, he can then consider whether placement in the

Enlightened Sentencing Project is appropriate. Most of the participants are poor, illiterate substance abusers living in the ghetto areas of St. Louis. These probationers are usually highly irregular in attending any programs that are made available to them, but that is not the case with the TM program.[12]

Judge Henry Autry, a member of the St. Louis judiciary who has been sentencing probationers to learn the TM technique, said:

> I have been using Transcendental Meditation as a condition of probation for over a year. And the results are astounding. I have seen my probationers who participate in the TM program grow and develop in ways I have rarely seen in other probationers. They have a positive social attitude. They secure employment. They exhibit responsibility by maintaining positive probation reports. And, as curious as it may sound, they have an emotionally healthy appearance. By this I mean that they do not appear to be stressed, anxious, nervous, or restless. These are responsible people with their lives under control as opposed to life controlling them. In short, they have taken responsibility for their lives. As I understand the purpose of probation, such a result is exactly what we in the criminal justice system seek to achieve.

Judge David Mason added:

> I have concluded that this program offers the most significant rehabilitative tool for offenders. The TM program reduces stress, and it does so more effectively than any other technique available. It is an excellent means to help someone achieve self-esteem, self-control, and resiliency from within.... Never before in our careers have we seen health benefits, families becoming stronger, and people's lives turning around this fast. Our results over the past two years have clearly confirmed the scientific research.

The St. Louis results, combined with the prison results overall in the U.S. and in other countries, are good evidence that the Vedic programs can work with virtually any individual in any culture. Dick Wright, who was the Assistant Superintendent of the Rutland, Vermont Correctional Institution, which also sponsored a Transcendental Meditation program for the inmates and staff, said:

> I think the biggest impact of the TM program for me is when I sit in a room with anywhere from two residents to thirty residents, and we practice the TM technique. No matter what happens after that, no matter what happened before that, with the residents, you know they all feel it; you know that they can all feel the unity and the power and that peacefulness. All of a sudden, everything is forgotten; all of a sudden there is no division between who you are and who they are. ■

NINE

Vedic Strategies to Foresee Dangerous Times

People from all walks of life have reported intuitions of things to come. Former Boston Celtics basketball star Bill Russell apparently often had such experiences. Russell said that every so often the game would become magical. He said when it happened, it would last anywhere from five minutes to a whole quarter or more and surround not only him and the other Celtics, but also the players on the other team and even the referees. He said that during these periods, he would almost sense how the next play would develop and where the next shot would be taken. He wanted to shout to his teammates, "It's coming there" except, he said, that he knew everything would change if he did. Russell said his intuitions were consistently correct.

This experience illustrates the value of intuition, of knowing on some subtle level what may be coming our way. Such experiences also indicate there are future tendencies that can be seen today. While most of us don't have intuitions of what may be on the horizon, there is an aspect of the Vedic knowledge, a predictive science known as *Jyotish* (referred to by some as Vedic astrology), that deals with identifying the principal signs of danger (or good fortune) that might be coming.

As You Sow, So Shall You Reap

Maharishi was once asked if it is possible to see the future. He said that seeing the future is just seeing the present more clearly, seeing the tree in the seed. As previously noted, the Vedic literature explains that our actions and even our thoughts generate influences in the environment, which reflect back on us (karma). Maharishi compares it to throwing a stone into a pond from the shore. The action produces a wave that travels throughout the pond, and once the wave reaches the far shore, it is reflected back to the point of origin. Like plucking a web at one point, the vibration radiates throughout the web, and then travels back to the original point. The question is whether there is some way that we can see what is coming toward us.

The principles of Jyotish as revived by Maharishi are known as *Maharishi Jyotish*[SM]. They tell us that our actions are like the seeds that we sow on a field. These actions are reflected throughout an interconnected universe. When the "seeds" have grown, the fruits of our actions are carried back to us by what are known as the *Grahas,* roughly translated as the planets.

The lack of seriousness with which many people treat the subject of astrology is primarily due to the many untrained, or improperly trained, so-called "experts" and from defects in systems of astrology that do not derive from the cognitions of the ancient Vedic sages. However, certain discoveries of modern science are beginning to change our conventional ideas about astrology, or at least about the Maharishi Jyotish program.

Dr. Nader, mentioned earlier for his discovery of the correspondence of the Vedic literature with the principal parts of the human physiology, has also discovered that the Vedic literature has a precise correspondence with the planets and other heavenly bodies.[1] Dr. Nader's research gives us a picture of how our good and bad actions come back to us in kind.

The Vedic Predictive Science

The Maharishi Jyotish program describes nine *Grahas* or planets—Sun, Moon, Mars, Mercury, Jupiter, Venus, Saturn, and two *lunar nodes*, known as Rahu and Ketu, which are the intersecting points of the orbits of the sun and moon as seen from Earth. Each of these Grahas is responsible for certain aspects of life, and corresponds to the portion of the nervous system affecting those areas of life. It is as if there is a transmitting station in the Grahas and a receiver in the human brain and nervous system.

Dr. Nader's research has discovered that each of the nine Grahas has an individual connection with a different part of the basal ganglia: thalamus, hypothalamus, etc.

Maharishi Jyotish: The Basal Ganglia and the 9 Grahas

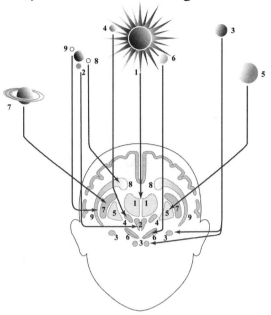

1· Surya or Sun	4· Budh or Mercury	7· Shani or Saturn
1· Thalamus	4· Subthalamus	7· Putamen
2· Chandra or Moon	5· Guru or Jupiter	8· Rahu or Ascending Lunar Node
2· Hypothalamus	5· Globus Pallidus	8· Nucleus Caudatus, head
3· Mangal or Mars	6· Shukra or Venus	9· Ketu or Descending Lunar Node
3· Amygdala	6· Substancia Nigra	9· Nucleus Caudatus, tail

This illustration shows a coronal section of the brain with its internal structures, including the basal ganglia, the thalamus, the hypothalamus, the subthalamus, etc., and their one-to-one relation to the nine Grahas (planets) of the solar system. The nine components of the internal structure of the brain have their counterparts in the solar system, and this accounts for the direct influence of the activity of the solar system on the human brain, and vice versa.

For example, the activity of our solar system centers around the sun, which has its counterpart in the thalamus. The thalamus occupies a central place in the brain, to which all the sensory inputs connect, just as the sun occupies the central place in the solar system, around which all the activity in our solar system revolves. The hypothalamus, according to Dr. Nader's research, has the moon as its cosmic counterpart. Both the moon and the hypothalamus are involved with emotions, as well as controlling reproductive behavior and various hormonal cycles.

Dr. Nader's research describes how each of the *nine* Grahas has its counterpart not only in the larger structures of the human brain and nervous system, but also in the *ninefold* internal structure of each cell in the body and the *nine* components of the DNA. The DNA, for example, revolves around a central axis made of hydrogen bonds. These hydrogen bonds correspond to the Sun (traditionally known in Vedic astrology as *Surya*). The heaviest constituent of DNA is guanine, which corresponds to Jupiter (known in the Vedic system as *Guru*), the heaviest planet. In the same way adenine corresponds to Saturn, cytosine to Mars, and so on.

Dr. Nader's research also shows that the 12 cranial nerves, based on their functions, directly correspond to the 12 signs in the zodiac and their traditional functions in Jyotish (see chart on next page), and the 27 groups of neurons in the brain stem have a one-to-one relationship to the 27 lunar constellations.[2] This research is continuing, but the planetary correspondence is too extensive to be simply a matter of chance. It appears that the correspondence of the stars to human physiology may be so precise that if there is some favorable aspect or debilitation in the individual's Jyotish chart, there is a reciprocal situation in the individual's physiology. For instance, when the sun is in an unfavorable position causing negative influences, based on the understandings of the Maharishi Jyotish program the thalamus may also be suffering from some affliction in that person's physiology.

The correspondence of the stars and the human physiology in part explains the influence of the stars on human activity. The planets are now seen as more than balls hanging around in space. The planets and constellations move in a certain mathematical way, which, according to Maharishi Jyotish, influences individuals, organizations, nations, and the world. People are actually influenced physiologically as their internal receptors receive messages from their heavenly counterparts (called "cosmic counterparts" by Maharishi). The Maharishi Jyotish program explains that we are born at a time and place that is optimal for delivering the karma of our past (i.e., the planets and other heavenly bodies are optimally aligned for this purpose).

Maharishi Jyotish: Cranial Nerves and the 12 Signs of the Vedic Zodiac

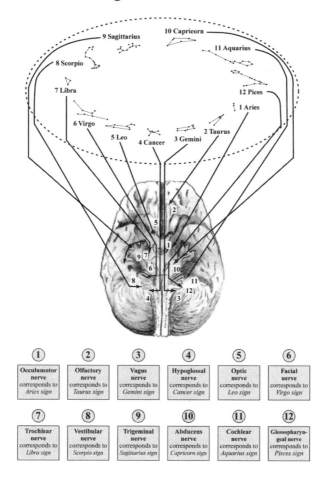

All illustrations in this chapter are reprinted, with permission, from Dr. Nader's book, *Human Physiology: Expressions of Veda and the Vedic Literature,* Maharishi Vedic University Press, Vlodrop, Holland, 1995.

Everyone experiences what appears to be a randomness in life bringing either good fortune or misfortune, early death or long life. However, the Vedic paradigm describes a highly mathematical precision to life's occurrences, arising from the interconnectedness of past, present, and future. Rather than events happening randomly, there is an underlying orderliness or intelligence of an unfathomable magnitude affecting the events in life. Most importantly, the movement and relationships of the stars can be calculated through the Vedic literature by the trained expert in the Maharishi Jyotish program. This allows him to determine when positive or harmful effects from the past will reach the individual.

The Vital Role of the *Maharishi Jyotish* Program

The Maharishi Jyotish program is part of the ancient Vedic tradition of knowledge and has stood the test of time. The trained Maharishi Jyotish expert can tell individuals about the nature and timing of significant events in their past, just from looking at their birth charts. If, without knowing anything about the individual, the Maharishi Jyotish expert can tell what type of illnesses the person has had and when those illnesses would have likely occurred; or the nature of his past relationships with a parent, spouse, or child; and, in general, the times in the past when there have been favorable or unfavorable events, it is apparent the birth chart must enable such information to be seen for the future. In other words, if you find that the expert accurately sees your past

> The correspondence of the stars to human physiology may be so precise that if there is some favorable aspect or debilitation in the individual's Jyotish chart, there is a reciprocal situation in the individual's physiology.

simply by analyzing your chart, it is a good indication that he can also see the tendencies in your future. The reading would have the same accuracy going forward or backwards from the time of the consultation.

Because the precise time of birth is very important to the ability to predict good or bad influences that may be coming, often the Maharishi Jyotish expert will first "rectify" or correct the birth time so that it corresponds to the major events in a person's life. In the past many hospitals did not accurately record the time of birth on the birth certificate. If the birth certificate gives a time of 2:15 A.M., the trained Maharishi Jyotish expert can see from the major events in one's life (the time of marriage, or the time of illnesses, or the date of the birth of a child, etc.) that the person's birth had to be at 1:53 A.M. for these events to have happened, not 2:15 A.M. as the birth certificate may indicate. Once the birth time is corrected, future predictions are more accurate.

Ken Leong studied to become a teacher in the Maharishi Jyotish training program. He responded to the concern that some people may have about knowing what may be coming by offering this explanation from Maharishi. Mr. Leong said:

> Jyotish is said to be the eyes of the Veda. Through Maharishi Jyotish we see what otherwise we could not see—we have a vision of the future. To say that we don't want to know what is coming in the future is like saying, "I want to be innocent when I'm driving on the road, so I'll keep my eyes closed." This is not a responsible view for ourselves or others on the road. We should know what is coming in life so that we can prevent problems.

According to the Maharishi Jyotish program, the *tendencies and influences* coming to us from the past, if not the precise events that are coming, can be calculated, and, importantly, if the time has not yet come for us to reap the effects of our actions, then we can improve the influence or offset it in whole or in part with a new influence. The direct way for the individual to enhance good influences and diminish the negative ones is by creating coherence in consciousness through the Transcendental Meditation and TM-Sidhi programs, including Yogic Flying. We gain support of nature by enlivening that higher intelligence in Natural Law, gaining what might be called Mother Nature's protective shield. But just as a mother cannot completely protect her children, the acts of the past are not completely neutralized.

In August 2002, a writer from Switzerland asked Maharishi whether his peace programs would wipe away all the consequences of bad conduct.

> Question: Do [your programs] mean that the destroyers of yesterday or today would not bear the consequences of their

actions in tomorrow's world of peace and harmony, or will there always be some turbulence in the world due to the actions of the past?

<u>Maharishi</u>: Actions must have their consequences. There is no hiding from it. Next day may be a bright day, but those who have broken their heads and knees in the darkness, they have to repair all that. When the world peace is going to be established through our efforts now, and we will have it very soon [depending on when we are able to have permanent Yogic Flying groups of a sufficient number], then all future trends and tendencies will be better and cordial and friendly and peaceful.

While past actions have their consequences, Maharishi is saying that the tendencies of the past can be mitigated. Maharishi Jyotish would be incomplete if we could not take some action to lessen or eliminate the bad actions that may be coming our way. The next chapter discusses the *Maharishi Yagya* program, the natural complement to the Maharishi Jyotish program. ■

TEN

Overcoming Danger
through Support
of Nature and Yagyas

The capacity of an individual to overcome previous harmful conduct, and to maximize his favorable tendencies, is measured by what Maharishi calls *support of nature*. Maharishi considers all wrongdoing to be a violation of some law of nature, which can therefore be overcome by enlisting the support of the laws of nature.

To illustrate support of nature, Maharishi tells a story of someone who wants an apple. At one level of support of nature, the man works all day, earns money, and buys an apple. But, when the laws of nature provide greater support for his activities, he just has the desire for an apple, and someone brings him an apple. Perhaps the crucial point in understanding support of nature is that everyone and everything is interconnected at the level of the transcendental field, which is found at the basis of human consciousness and at the basis of all of nature. When an individual functions from the level of the transcendental field, nature's functioning supports individual desires.

In his book, *Bhagavad-Gita, A New Translation and Commentary, Chapters 1–6* (the Bhagavad-Gita is a key text in the Vedic literature), Maharishi explains that the transcendental field forms the basis of creation and therefore upholds the universe. During the practice of the Transcendental Meditation technique, the individual experiences the transcendental field, the Unified Field of Natural Law (the field of higher intelligence permeating everything). As the individual continues to meditate, he increasingly functions from that most powerful level of life that connects everyone and everything. When the mind gains the status of the transcendental field, the individual gains the support of all of nature to effortlessly fulfill his desires and to increasingly shield him from harm.

In his commentary on the *Bhagavad Gita*, Maharishi offers an analogy to help understand support of nature. He states:

> When during Transcendental Meditation, the mind transcends the subtlest state of thought...it attains the level of cosmic law [the level where the laws of nature support the entire cosmos]. Coming out of that state, its position is like that of a man entering the office of the President and coming out endowed with his goodwill; all the subordinates begin to be in sympathy with him and give him their full support by directing his activities toward a successful end.

> When the mind comes out from the plane of cosmic law, into the relative field of activity, which is under the influence of innumerable laws of nature, it automatically enjoys the support of the cosmic law, and this makes possible the accomplishment of any aspiration and the ultimate fulfillment of life.[1]

Individual Support of Nature

Six weeks after the 9/11 attack, we talked to Euripedes (Rip) Karydas, a traffic engineer for the New York Port Authority. He had been in charge of ground transportation at JFK International Airport, but his principal offices on September 11, 2001, were on the 73rd floor of the north tower at the World Trade Center. He credits the Transcendental Meditation and Maharishi Yagya programs (described later in this chapter) for the increasing support of nature in his life. Mr. Karydas said:

> On September 11, I was supposed to go to the World Trade Center to pick up a car in the garage area below the building and then drive it out to JFK airport. For some reason, I was procrastinating, and was late leaving my apartment. So instead I decided to go directly to my satellite office at Kennedy airport. This was an unusual decision, totally outside the scope of my normal work experience, and I was even

puzzled by it. Instead of being in the World Trade Center, I was at Kennedy airport when the first plane crashed into the building.

Support of nature is a common experience shared by millions of people in the world. Support of nature can be thought of as having thoughts or desires that put us in the right place at the right time, or at least not in the wrong place; or simply as having the fulfillment of some desire, or when some good fortune comes our way. Everyone at times has support of nature, and there are thousands of stories of good fortune in the accounts, for example, of all those with offices in the World Trade Center who survived the September 11 attack. However, the experience of those who learn the Transcendental Meditation technique is that good fortune—support of nature—is enhanced as they increasingly, and spontaneously, learn to function from the transcendental field.

Maharishi Yagya^{SM} **Performances**

The Maharishi Yagya program is an integral part of Vedic defense. For centuries, the Vedic tradition has utilized special recitations of

> Maharishi Yagya performances are traditionally understood to help prevent war and violence in a city or in the nation.

Vedic sounds to help gain support of nature and to minimize or overcome misfortune. These sounds and the manner in which they are recited are called Yagya performances. Every Maharishi Yagya performance has a goal of accomplishing a specific result or fulfilling a specific desire, and the performance begins with a resolution of the goal to be accomplished. Some of the performances are for removing obstacles from business transactions, while others improve specific health disorders, protect against accidents, or support harmonious family relationships. Still other Maharishi Yagya performances are traditionally understood to help prevent war and violence in a city or in the nation by enlivening the harmonious aspects of Natural Law and neutralizing the destructive aspects.

During the Maharishi Yagya performances, the trained Vedic pandits recite specific mantras or verses from certain books of the Vedic literature, including Rik Veda, Sama Veda, Yajur-Veda, and Atharva Veda. These recitations create sound waves that have an effect on the subtlest levels of the human physiology. Because of the correspondence of the human physiology with its cosmic counterparts (see Chapter 9), the sounds create reverberations in the corresponding cosmic counterparts (the Grahas or planets), improving the intimate relationship between the individual and the cosmos. The effect is to enhance the good influences or diminish the bad influences that are foreseen by the trained expert in the Maharishi Jyotish program.

Vedic pandits preparing for Maharishi Yagya performances.

The Yagya performances from Maharishi's Vedic tradition are set procedures that have not been invented by anyone, but, like the entire Vedic literature, are known by direct cognition. Enlightened Vedic sages cognized the precise recitations that enhance the relationship of the individual physiology to the cosmic counterparts, and even the best times to utilize Maharishi Yagya performances. There are days in the Vedic calendar when it is more optimal to conduct the performances so that they will achieve their predicted results. In addition, one of Maharishi's principal contributions in this area is the realization that Yagyas must be performed by the Vedic pandits from a coherent state of consciousness in order to have the predicted effect. This is why Maharishi's pandits practice the

Transcendental Meditation technique and the Yogic Flying program, which allows them to develop a more coherent (higher) state of consciousness. In his commentary on the Bhagavad-Gita, Maharishi explains:

> The Vedas prescribe certain ritualistic performances by certain competent people to produce certain life-supporting influences in nature. This also results in gaining the sympathy of the laws of nature by creating an influence of harmony in the atmosphere and maintaining the rhythm of nature, so that [for example] rain comes in due time for the production of food....
>
> The more gross aspect of Yagya, that is, performance of rites and ritual... for the sake of material well-being, needs action in the gross field of life for its accomplishment. Likewise, the more subtle aspect of Yagya, which is the process of contacting the transcendental [field] needs action in the subtle fields. This action in the subtle aspect of life is the process of Transcendental Meditation, whereby the mind travels through all the subtler levels of existence and transcends the subtlest level of manifested life [a thought] to reach the state of absolute Being [the transcendental field].[2]

One of Maharishi's programs to eliminate terrorism involves a particular Maharishi Yagya performance, known as the *Ati Rudrabhishek Maha Yagya*. This will be performed several times each day by the Vedic pandits to be assembled in the U.S., and the 40,000 pandits planned for India. Maharishi Yagya performances to produce a particular result for an individual often do not require a large group recitation. However, influencing the collective consciousness of the world to prevent terrorism on a global scale requires a sizeable group. The effect of the Maha Yagya (*Maha* means great) by a group, like the effect of the group Yogic Flying program, is also based on the square of the number in the group. In other words, the 40,000-pandit Maharishi Yagya project in India is expected to have the effect of 1.6 billion pandits separately engaged in the Yagya performances.

Some of the 200,000 students at Maharishi Schools in India.
Many will train to become Vedic pandits.

Dr. Bevan Morris, president of Maharishi University of Management and one of Maharishi's principal administrators and spokespersons for more than 30 years, discussed the Maharishi Jyotish and Maharishi Yagya programs at a press conference in the summer of 2002. Dr. Morris said:

> The Vedic pandits...through their training in transcending and experiencing transcendental consciousness will also be performing certain Vedic Yagya performances for peace. When the Vedic pandits use specific sounds as in the *Ati Rudrabhishek Maha Yagya*, they enliven the infinite silence or infinite peace quality in world consciousness....
>
> Furthermore, within the group of 40,000 in India, there will be Vedic pandits assigned to each country on earth. And they will have the *Kundali* or birth chart of that nation, through which it will be possible for the Maharishi Jyotish experts to predict when there is oncoming danger to any nation. And when

there is such danger, the pandits will perform specific Vedic acts, *Graha Shanti* it is called, performance of *Yagyas*, to avert the danger that has not yet come for those nations.

The Program to Prevent Terrorism

The principal aspect of the Vedic program to prevent terrorism in the U.S. involves 8,000 American Yogic Flyers supported by a core group of 500 Vedic pandits in the U.S., along with a 40,000-pandit group planned for India. The American Yogic Flyers will largely be the student body at Maharishi Vedic Universities, and the largest number of students is expected to be located at a Vedic University campus in Maharishi Vedic City in Iowa.

The 500 pandits in the U.S. will spend each day practicing the Vedic technologies of consciousness, principally the Transcendental Meditation technique and the Yogic Flying program, and performing Yagyas. Maharishi Yagya performances are considered to be no less important than Yogic Flying in preventing terrorism, even though not yet as well researched by modern science.

Several times each day the pandits will perform the *Ati Rudrabhishek Maha Yagya* to prevent war and international conflict. In addition, as indicated by Dr. Morris, separate Maharishi Yagya performances will be conducted for every nation to protect each nation from terrorist activity. The Maharishi Jyotish experts will prescribe specific Maharishi Yagya performances for a nation, based on the precise time the nation was legally formed.

The principal element in developing an immediate defense against terrorism is *Rastriya Kavatch*, the creation of an invincible armor of defense through the group practice of Yogic Flying and group Yagya performances by Maharishi's experts. In the ideal situation, however, Maharishi's programs would be utilized to help everyone develop consciousness for their own health and prosperity, while at the same time contributing to world harmony. ■

ELEVEN

The Moral Brain

From the perspective of the terrorist, his attacks, even on noncombatants, are not immoral. Osama bin Laden is a religious fanatic, bent on what he sees as a Holy War, and he justifies the killing of "infidels" on religious grounds. A similar "moral" justification for killing is apparent in history's most infamous terrorist, Adolf Hitler. His policy of Aryan supremacy was designed to result in the worldwide dominion of the "pure" German race. To accomplish his goals he burned "immoral books" in his police state, and killed over 6,000,000 European Jews. In Timothy McVeigh we also see an example of mass destruction as a "moral" retaliation for perceived unrighteousness. In 1995, he bombed the Alfred P. Murrah federal building in Oklahoma City after being greatly disturbed by two events: the Waco, Texas, Branch Davidian standoff resulting in the Waco inferno in 1993, and the 1992 shoot-out between federal agents and a co-survivalist, Randy Weaver, resulting in Weaver's wife and child being killed. The Murrah federal building that he bombed was the main office of the federal agents involved in the Waco standoff.

Jessica Stern, in her book *The Ultimate Terrorist*,[1] describes the moral justification that often leads to terrorist acts of mass destruction. Terrorists, she says, imagine themselves as threatened by a great evil. Islamic extremists label the United States as the *Great Satan*, and refer to their enemies generally as the "infidel." Neo-Nazi hate groups refer to African-Americans as the "children of darkness," and to Jews as a "virus," while Aryans are described as "pure," and the "children of light."

In cultures that condone violence as a means to a religious objective, those who engage in terrorist acts are considered heroes. Dr. Harvey W. Kushner, an expert in terrorism and Chairman of the Department of Criminal Justice at Long Island University, says that suicide bombers see their actions as for the greater good of society.[2] Dr. Clark McCauley, professor of psychology at Bryn Mawr College, says that in some societies suicide bombers are not different from members of any fighting group who are trained to sacrifice their own welfare for the common good.[3]

In cultures that make heroes out of terrorist martyrs, and in light of the religious or ideological fanaticism of the terrorist, there is nothing that can intellectually dissuade a terrorist from detonating his device. However, while he is beyond the reach of persuasion, he is not beyond the reach of the *spontaneous and automatic* development of moral behavior that results from the transcendent experience. From the Vedic perspective, moral education is not primarily a matter of teaching the rules of proper moral conduct (for instance, teaching that killing in the name of religion is immoral), or establishing politically democratic regimes. As Maharishi explains, Vedic science holds that a more coherent consciousness (caused by regular experiences of the transcendent state) and its physical counterpart, coherent brain functioning, *necessarily leads to greater moral behavior.*

This is an entirely new paradigm. We have spiritual leaders today who have gained their status based on years of religious education, or on their ability to appeal to a television audience, but this does not necessarily have anything to do with the spiritual leader's actual brain functioning or the level of coherence in consciousness, which according to Vedic science is the real basis of spirituality.

Higher Consciousness and Higher Values

Interviews with business people have strongly suggested that the natural development brought about by the TM technique necessarily develops both ethical and material values. Mark Horvath, director of Selecta International, a food marketing company headquartered in England, reported:

> Take action you know to be wrong and you won't find that action successful—you won't be able to make it work properly.... Or try being dishonest, and even if you thought in the past that your conscience would let you get away with that sort of thing, you find now, after meditating for a while, you can't do it without making yourself feel rotten.[4]

There is nothing new about the principle that a more developed consciousness is accompanied by higher values. In every age the world's great philosophers have noted that honorable and high-minded qualities, with their higher concerns and noble values, were natural qualities of men and women with a developed consciousness. Confucius said, "The superior man thinks always of virtue; the common man thinks of comfort." Aristotle said, "Honor and dishonor are the matters with which the high-minded man is especially concerned." Sir Francis Bacon said, "There is a great difference between a cunning man and a wise man, not only in point of honesty but in point of ability… and nothing doth more hurt in a State than that cunning men pass for wise."

We have simply not yet appreciated that a more developed consciousness means more coherence in the mind and in brain functioning.

The Moral Brain

Significant research has now shown that the inability to make proper moral decisions is connected to brain functioning. As one example, researchers at the University of Iowa College of Medicine studied 57 subjects and found that brain-damaged individuals displayed defective decision making (especially in the social realm), a striking lack of insight, a general dampening of emotional experience, poor judgment, and poor frustration tolerance, among other defects.[5] Other studies show that following trauma to the right frontal regions of the brain, the subject acquires many sociopathic tendencies marked by high levels of aggression and a callous disregard for others. An especially interesting study shows that moral decision making is located in particular areas of the brain. Using magnetic resonance imaging techniques, researchers were able to look at images of the brain while the subjects evaluated morally charged statements as being either "right" or "wrong," and, for comparison, were also presented with statements that had no moral content. The researchers found that their results concurred with clinical observations assigning a critical role for the frontal poles and right anterior temporal cortex in making judgments about moral matters. More recent research found a network of brain structures (medial orbital, frontal cortex, temporal pole, and the superior temporal sulcus of the left hemisphere) was activated by moral judgments.[6]

It appears that when these parts of the brain do not activate appropriately, whether due to trauma or other disability, the subject will express defects in his capacity for moral judgments, a lack of empathy, and callous behavior.

Using the Brain's Hidden Reserves

Professor N.N. Lyubimov of the Moscow Brain Research Institute of the Russian Academy of Medical Sciences, one of the world's foremost neuroscientists, conducted brain research for years on humans and animals who were ill or had various incapacities or personality disorders. His research showed that there were "hidden reserves" in the brain that could potentially be activated enabling people to heal themselves by using these different pathways, even when part of the brain was traumatized. Dr. Lyubimov learned about the Transcendental Meditation program in the mid-1980s and visited Maharishi's headquarters in Holland to conduct research. Dr. Lyubimov's research on long-term practitioners of the Transcendental Meditation technique revealed the mechanism that may be responsible for the wide-ranging beneficial effects of the technique on complex mental processes associated with learning and moral judgments.

> We have spiritual leaders today who have gained their status based on years of religious education, or on their ability to appeal to a television audience, but this does not necessarily have anything to do with the spiritual leader's actual brain functioning or the level of coherence in consciousness, which according to Vedic science is the real basis of spirituality.

Mobilization of the Latent Reserves of the Brain through the *TM* Technique

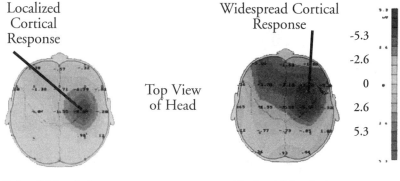

Localized Cortical Response

Widespread Cortical Response

Top View of Head

-5.3

-2.6

0

2.6

5.3

Before TM technique

During TM technique

This study found that during the Transcendental Meditation program some of the early sensory components of the brain's response to somatosensory stimulation (0–100 msec) are more widely distributed across the cortex. This study, by Dr. Nicolai Nicolaevich Lyubimov, Director of the Moscow Brain Research Institute's Laboratory of Neurocybernetics, indicated that during the Transcendental Meditation program there is an increase in the areas of the cortex taking part in perception of specific information and an increase in the functional relationship between the two hemispheres.

Dr. Lyubimov found that when the meditators were simply sitting with their eyes closed prior to beginning the Transcendental Meditation technique, a slight stimulus applied to the hand and arm would evoke the normal response which could be localized in a particular area of the brain. To Dr. Lyubimov's surprise, during the practice of the TM technique, when the stimulus was applied to the meditator, the electrical response of the brain was consistently distributed much more widely over the cerebral cortex than was customary, indicating that TM is a dynamic process utilizing more areas of the brain than during normal waking activity. Dr. Lyubimov concluded that the brain wakes up during the practice of the

> When these parts of the brain do not activate appropriately, the subject will express defects in his capacity for moral judgments.

147

Transcendental Meditation technique, seeming to allow the individual, after his meditation program, to use hidden reserves of the brain to make complex moral and other judgments that previously were not possible.[7]

Research on Moral Judgment

A number of studies on students at Maharishi University of Management in Fairfield, Iowa, show the relationship of their meditation practice to increased moral development and pro-social behavior. All the students at the University at both the undergraduate and graduate levels practice the Transcendental Meditation technique.

In early research that I (Dr. Wallace) participated in with Dr. Sanford Nidich, we attempted to determine whether EEG brain wave coherence was associated with pro-social behavior. In our initial study[8] we evaluated 30 graduate students in the masters in education program, 13 of whom were rated as *highly* pro-social individuals. This is a distinction made in the field of social psychology based primarily on finding that these individuals were on the "leading edge" of the group, and that their behavior enhanced the overall coherence and interaction of the members of the class. They made constructive and uplifting comments to the professor and class members, showed an absence of negativity in their speech and behavior, inspired others to follow the group norms, and showed a sincere desire to improve society. The comparison group was friendly and interacted well with others, but they did not exhibit highly pro-social behavior. The results of the research showed that the EEG coherence in the frontal area of the brain was importantly related to pro-social behavior, irrespective of the student's grade point average or age.

In another study of 76 undergraduate students it was found that the practice of the TM-Sidhi program (including Yogic Flying) results in higher levels of principled moral thinking than in those practicing the Transcendental Meditation program alone.[9]

A study on high school students at the Maharishi School of the Age of Enlightenment in Fairfield, Iowa, where all students practice the Transcendental Meditation technique, showed an unusually high moral atmosphere in the school, something its administrators had known for years. The collective consciousness responsible for the school's unusual atmosphere was measured using what are known as "dilemma interviews" developed at Harvard's Center for Moral Education. Questions posing significant moral dilemmas were developed by leading researchers to determine the moral atmosphere in schools or other institutions. The study compared two groups: students who had transferred to the Maharishi School from other schools, and students from the schools the Maharishi School students had previously attended. The reports indicated that in their choices and behavior, the subjects who had transferred to the Maharishi School and learned the Transcendental Meditation technique reported that they would make pro-social choices in 95% of the cases, compared to the non-meditating students who had not transferred who made pro-social choices in only 36% of the cases. The Maharishi School students reported taking the community needs into account in making decisions in 73% of the cases, whereas it was estimated that the non-meditating students on average would take community needs into account in approximately 20% of the situations. The study found that the TM program was the major contributing factor in the extremely high level of moral atmosphere at the Maharishi School. The number of years practicing the TM program was also relevant. In general, the longer the individuals had been meditating, the greater the pro-social behavior, a further indication that the TM program was responsible for the change.[10]

Along with the moral development resulting from the practice of the TM technique, students at the Maharishi School display an exceptionally high level of success in school activities. They win or place in the state tennis tournament virtually every year, and excel in basketball, soccer, golf, and other sports, as well as in drama, art, and academics (several years ago one-fourth of the senior class, 11 out of 41 students, were either National Merit Scholar finalists or commended Merit Scholars). It is evident that development of consciousness brings moral development *and* success in daily activities.

Finally, in a study conducted at the University of Cincinnati on the TM program and moral values[11], a psychologist administered Kohlberg's Moral Judgment interview to 96 student meditators at Maharishi

University of Management and to 30 non-meditator students at the University of Cincinnati. The study used Kohlberg's hierarchy of moral levels of development, which places a person at a particular level of moral development based on the reasons they give for engaging in a certain activity.

For example, if you believe that it is right to keep a promise, your reasons indicate your level of moral maturity. At one level, you may keep a promise because of the possibly unpleasant physical consequences for not doing so. At a slightly higher level, you may keep a promise for reasons of mutual benefit—"You scratch my back and I'll scratch yours." At another level, you may value the maintenance of the social order for its own sake. At still another level, you define right action by a decision of conscience in accordance with principles of justice, equality, and respect for individual dignity. Partly because the classifications are so sophisticated, the interviews in this study were all sent to the Harvard University Moral Development Center to be scored by experts.

Statistical analysis of the study confirmed that the moral maturity of meditating students was more highly developed than that of the non-meditators. The meditators exhibited *significantly* higher levels of moral development in their thinking. Their attitude was not merely "conformity to... social order, but loyalty to it, of actively maintaining, supporting, and justifying the order, and of identifying with the person or group involved in it." The non-meditators exhibited significantly more "preconventional thinking," a lesser state of development in which wrong depends merely on the physical consequences of action (reward, punishment, exchange of favors) or on the physical power of those who issue the rules.

Holistic Development

In the East, meditation of any kind has long been appreciated as a procedure for gaining enlightenment, but gaining enlightenment is often understood to be an exclusively spiritual pursuit. In fact, practical worldly pursuits are usually considered an obstacle to enlightenment. Moreover, most believe that very few can succeed. This Eastern *misunderstanding* of the path to enlightenment underemphasizes worldly responsibilities in the name of spirituality.

In the West, on the other hand, there is little appreciation of the development of higher values through meditation. Here, the TM technique is understood primarily as a technique for relaxation, which may also enhance material success and enjoyment. It is rarely, if ever, recognized as promoting higher values or any spiritual development because, after all, how could more orderly brain wave activity or activating dormant areas of the brain result in greater morality or spirituality? In the U.S. particularly, the

> Moral behavior is dependent on the development of consciousness; it is not based on individuals or groups learning new rules of moral behavior.

word "spirituality" itself tends to be confused with religion, but spiritual development from the TM program is just one aspect of the natural development of consciousness and brain functioning.

How did these misunderstandings develop? Maharishi explains that there were originally two separate types of meditation. One was for the recluse, or monk, and the other was for the active person with family responsibilities. As time passed the former was preserved in monasteries, while the latter (the TM technique as taught to the public) was evidently lost, accounting for the popular impression that meditation leads to a life of withdrawal.

Maharishi's understanding of human evolution and the mechanics of the TM technique allowed him to interpret the most important texts of the Vedic literature in a way that had not been understood by scholars anywhere. For example, his commentary on the Bhagavad-Gita[12] demonstrates that the Gita's repeated references to the need for withdrawal to gain higher values and enlightenment refer not to a reclusive way of life but to the effortless withdrawal from all activity and all thoughts, which occurs in the simplest state of consciousness that occurs during meditation.

In reviving the TM technique, Maharishi has thus restored the understanding that an active person can effectively develop an integrated life of both higher values and material fulfillment. Maharishi has also corrected the mistaken belief that renunciation and withdrawal are the primary means of developing higher values. Seen in this light, "spiritual growth" through the TM program just means the growth of consciousness, supported by integrated brain development.

Most importantly for purposes of this book, there is a spontaneous quality of right and moral behavior that naturally develops as individual consciousness develops. Moral behavior is dependent on the development of consciousness; it is not based on individuals or groups learning new rules of moral behavior. Someone who walks past a jewelry store that has been left unlocked in the evening may entertain thoughts about entering the store, taking what he can, and leaving. At a higher level of consciousness, the only thoughts that are entertained relate to calling the police or store owner to help avoid a burglary. The development of consciousness spontaneously enhances moral thoughts and actions, and a moral atmosphere results from the development of the collective consciousness. ■

TWELVE

Maharishi Vedic City in Iowa: A Model City for the World

The Vedic peace technologies are currently being applied in Iowa's newest city, Maharishi Vedic City, which is adjacent to Fairfield, Iowa, the home of Maharishi University of Management. Beginning in the mid-1970s, several thousand TM meditators moved to Fairfield, relocating there when it was discovered how much more powerful it was to practice the Transcendental Meditation and Yogic Flying programs as a group. In the summer of 2001 their efforts resulted in the formation of Maharishi Vedic City.

With plans to generate harmonious living and great support of nature based on Maharishi's Vedic peace technologies, Maharishi Vedic City already has over 125 new residences, medical clinics, hotels, and office buildings, all designed in accordance with the Vedic system of architecture (see below).

Capital of the Global Country for World Peace in Maharishi Vedic City, Iowa

The residents of Maharishi Vedic City are all TM meditators and Yogic Flyers, and when the city was formed the first acts of the mayor and City Council were to adopt the Constitution of Iowa, the Constitution of the U.S., and the Constitution of the Universe—the primordial sounds that form the fundamental blueprint of creation—as the city's guiding principles.

This is a city unlike any other in America. Everything in the city is Vedic, and, as such, it serves as a model city for the world. All the buildings, roads, green space, and herbal and floral gardens are structured in accordance with Vedic principles of design (see below). Several hotels offer extensive programs for chronic disease based on the Maharishi Vedic Approach to Health℠, and the city has developed a large agricultural project (also described below) producing Maharishi Vedic Organic™ foods for sale and for the nourishment of the University students.

Vedic Architecture

In India, in Maharishi Vedic City, and elsewhere in the U.S. where the Vedic pandits and Maharishi Vedic University students will be located, buildings are being constructed according to the Vedic principles of architecture known as *Sthapatya Veda*. This knowledge has been revived in its completeness by Maharishi and is known as *Maharishi Sthapatya Veda*℠ design. This ancient system of architecture specifies how buildings should be designed in order to bring maximum coherence to the individual and the environment. The regular practice of the Yogic Flying program and the Maharishi Yagya performances in buildings that are designed according to the Vedic specifications will intensify the effects of these programs.

Sthapatya Veda is the most ancient system of country, city, village, and residence planning in accordance with those laws of nature that connect the individual to his surroundings and to his cosmic counterparts (the planets and other heavenly bodies). The Vedic architectural principles have the purpose of establishing one's home, city, and country in perfect alliance with the environment and with Natural Law, that higher intelligence in nature. Maharishi has repeatedly emphasized that if our homes and working places are not in harmony with the laws of nature that maintain order in the universe, the life of the individual will remain imbalanced, leading to ill health, problems, and misfortune. Houses and offices not constructed in accord with the laws of nature create anxiety, depression, chronic disease, bad luck, financial losses, disharmony in relationships, antisocial behavior, and even violent tendencies. The Vedic design principles, on the other hand, promote health, success, and improved relationships for the inhabitants of the buildings.

Vedic residence of Ed Malloy, mayor of Fairfield, Iowa

The Rukmapura Park Hotel in Maharishi Vedic City, Iowa

One of the most important principles of building in harmony with Natural Law is positioning the building in the right direction with respect to the path of the sun. The Vedic principles prescribe that the entrance to a building face east, while entrances to the south are considered to be the least auspicious, bringing various negative influences to the inhabitants. There are other essential elements including the proper Vedic proportion and location of each room, as well as elements recognized by modern building sciences, including non-toxic construction, generous light, fresh air, and generous green space.

Aerial view of 45 Maharishi Sthapatya Veda buildings in Maharishi Vedic City. These will house 500 Vedic pandit students from India.

All the roads and infrastructure of Maharishi Vedic City have been designed to maximize the support of nature for the city's inhabitants. The orderly design of such a city, including all building entrances facing east, is vastly different from how the major cities in the world have been constructed. Maharishi has described how much of the chaos, ill health, and crime in city life is unnecessary and has its roots in the faulty layout and structure of the roads and houses, which invite disruptive influences.

Maharishi Gandharva Veda^{SM} **Music**

An integral part of the Vedic peace technologies employs Vedic sounds or melodies to enliven coherence and help overcome problems caused by past violations of the laws of nature. Over the past 15 or so years, Maharishi has revived the knowledge of *Gandharva Veda*, which is understood in Vedic science as the music of nature. If we could hear the subtle changing frequencies present in nature in the first awakening of the dawn, the

> With the Bach organ music, the plants inclined 35 degrees toward the music, which seemed unprecedented, until the plants bent more than 60 degrees in an effort to approach the Vedic music.

dynamism of midday, and the silence of midnight, we would be hearing the frequencies of Gandharva Veda music.

The subtle rhythms and melodies of Maharishi Gandharva Veda music correspond to the vibrations and frequencies in nature at a particular time of the day. The Vedic music restores biological rhythms by attuning the individual physiology to the cycles of nature. There is particular Maharishi Gandharva Veda music that is played in the evening, for example, just before bed to attune the physiology with the resting cycle of nature and promote a healthy night's sleep. Playing these melodies also has the effect of restoring balance in the resting cycle in the whole environment. There are also Maharishi Gandharva Veda melodies that address particular disorders in the individual and in the society.

While the use of sound as a means of healing the body or promoting harmony in the society is well understood in Maharishi Vedic Science^{SM}, its use for such purposes is not widely understood by modern science. There are, however, a number of interesting studies that hint at the potential effects.

In *The Sound of Music and Plants*, Dorothy Retallack details her plant experiments at the Colorado Women's College in Denver.[1] Ms. Retallack demonstrated that plants exposed to soothing "middle of the road" music for three hours each day grew healthy and their stems began bending toward the music, whereas the plants that were played rock music grew gangly with small leaves and had their growth stunted. By the 16th day, all but a few of the plants in the rock music chamber were dying.

Over time, Ms. Retallack experimented with different types of music, including jazz, Bach organ music, as well as classical Indian Gandharva Veda music. Ms. Retallack discovered that the plants responded most favorably to the Gandharva Veda music. With the Bach organ music, the plants inclined 35 degrees toward the music, which seemed unprecedented, until the plants bent more than 60 degrees in an effort to approach the Vedic music.[2]

The reason that plant life benefits most from Vedic sounds is that, as Maharishi explains, the sounds of the Vedic literature are not just extremely harmonious sounds, but are actually the primordial sounds that give rise to the structure of all matter, including plant life *and* human life.

The Vedic sounds are expressed in the ancient Sanskrit language, and the Sanskrit expressions themselves produce increased coherence in consciousness for those listening to or reciting the expressions. Research recently published in the *International Journal of Neuroscience* shows that some of the physiological effects from reading Sanskrit are similar to those experienced during the Transcendental Meditation technique. Dr. Fred Travis, who conducted the study, had 18 subjects read a passage in Sanskrit and in modern foreign languages (Spanish, French, or German). In each case the subjects could pronounce the sounds, but didn't know the meaning. Dr. Travis measured EEG, heart rate, breath rate, and skin conductance during the Sanskrit sessions, during the reading of other foreign languages, and during a 15-minute session of the Transcendental Meditation technique. He found that the patterns of skin conductance levels and EEG power and coherence while reading Sanskrit indicated a highly relaxed and coherent state, and were significantly different from reading the other languages.

Maharishi Vedic Organic Agriculture^{SM}

Maharishi Vedic Organic Agriculture produces organic food that is enriched by playing the Vedic sounds to bring the plants the support of the higher intelligence of Natural Law. The Vedic sounds used in Maharishi's agricultural program are organized so that at each stage of the plant's growth suitable melodies are played to bring about the full blossoming of that stage of development.

In addition, plants not only respond to sound, but also respond to the influence of those who care for the plants. In Maharishi's programs the farmers not only take care of the crops, they also take care of their own consciousness through the Vedic procedures, thereby providing a further nourishing effect on the plants. The life-supporting influence of the Vedic sounds, and of the Vedic farmer's own thought, speech, and action, serve as a fertilizer for the plants and their ability to promote health and proper thinking in those who eat these products.

The organic farm in Maharishi Vedic City includes a projected 100-acre greenhouse operation in which vegetables are grown year-round using the Vedic methods. Crops are picked when they have ripened naturally, and are sold within a 300-mile radius of the city to ensure freshness and potency.

Vedic Health Care

Maharishi Vedic Approach to Health provides knowledge and programs that are crucial to maintaining health and the development of consciousness. As mentioned earlier, the foundation of this approach are the Transcendental Meditation and TM-Sidhi programs, including Yogic Flying, which promote ideal health from its basis—pure consciousness. Both short- and long-term health benefits of the Transcendental Meditation program and the advanced Yogic Flying program have been well researched.

Many studies over the years have shown dramatic decreases in health care cost in TM meditators, including finding 87% decreased hospitalization for heart disease; 55% less illness for cancer; 87% less illness for nervous system disorders; and 73% less illness for nose, throat, and lung problems.[3]

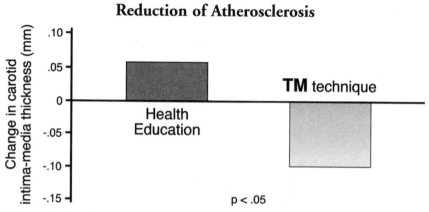

Reduction of Atherosclerosis

This study found that those who learned the Transcendental Meditation program, indicated on the right bar, showed reduced thickening of the carotid artery. This finding was in contrast to continued thickening of this artery among a control group, shown on the left, who took a health education program on diet and exercise for alleviating cardiovascular problems.

Reference: *Stroke* 31 (2000): 568-573

Perhaps the most convincing evidence for the application of the Transcendental Meditation and TM-Sidhi programs in the area of health comes from studies supported by the National Institutes of Health, which have provided funding of more than $18 million for research on the use of the Transcendental Meditation program to reduce high blood pressure and heart disease. Heart disease is the number one killer in the United States, and in most technologically advanced countries. Since numerous universities are competing for the National Institutes' resources, only the most carefully designed studies are funded.

Improved Health in Industrial Workers

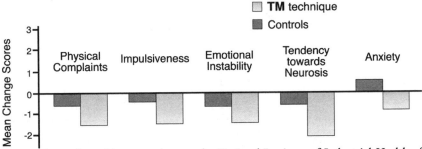

In a study conducted by researchers at the National Institute of Industrial Health of the Japanese Ministry of Labor and the St. Marianna Medical Institute, 447 industrial workers of Sumitomo Heavy Industries were taught the Transcendental Meditation technique and compared with 321 workers who did not learn the practice. The Transcendental Meditation technique group showed significantly decreased physical complaints, decreased impulsiveness, decreased emotional instability, decreased neurotic tendencies, decreased anxiety, and also decreased insomnia.

References:
1. *Japanese Journal of Industrial Health* 32 (1990): 656
2. *Japanese Journal of Public Health* 37 (1990): 729

Studies conducted by Dr. Robert Schneider and co-researchers have been published in top medical journals, and clearly show the value of the Transcendental Meditation program in reducing high blood pressure and in helping to relieve heart disease.[5] Not only does this represent a dramatic saving in cost, compared to the use of modern medicines, but unlike the pharmacological approach to treating hypertension, using the Transcendental Meditation program creates absolutely no adverse side effects.

It should be noted that there are advocates of meditation who generalize that all meditation programs produce the same or similar results, and then cite the research on the Transcendental Meditation program in an effort to validate their own programs.[5] However, those who have looked carefully find that the practical benefits of the Transcendental Meditation program have not been duplicated by other techniques of meditation or other relaxation programs. One particularly good comparative study involved an analysis of 99 studies (146 outcomes) comparing the Transcendental Meditation technique to other meditation or relaxation techniques. The findings were that the TM technique produced significantly greater effects—in fact, approximately twice the effect of techniques of relaxation.[6]

Reduced Anxiety through the TM Technique

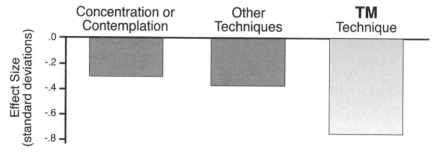

A statistical meta-analysis conducted at Stanford University of all available studies (146 independent outcomes) indicated that the effect of the Transcendental Meditation program on reducing trait anxiety was much greater than that of concentration or contemplation or other techniques. Analysis showed that these positive results could not be attributed to subject expectation, experimenter bias, or quality of research design.
References:
1. *Journal of Clinical Psychology* 45 (1989): 957-974
2. *Journal of Clinical Psychology* 33 (1977): 1076-1078

The principal U.S. center for the Maharishi Vedic Approach to Health is located in Maharishi Vedic City at The Raj Hotel.

The Maharishi Vedic Approach to Health also uses extensive knowledge of traditional Vedic pulse diagnosis, herbal treatments, purification procedures for the physiology, and the Maharishi Jyotish and Yagya programs, with their knowledge of how the planets affect health and how to neutralize negative influences. The most advanced aspect of Maharishi's health care program involves the use of Vedic sounds to restore balance in the body. This program uses the Vedic sounds as a means of re-enlivening the correct, sequential flow of information in the body to correct disorders, reestablish health, and support the development of consciousness. All aspects of the Vedic knowledge, including the Vedic approaches to health, architecture, and agriculture, contribute to the coherence in the collective consciousness of the society, the antidote to terrorist acts of mass destruction according to the Vedic perspective. ∎

THIRTEEN

Preventing the Birth of an Enemy

> "[In war] once you hear the details of victory, it is hard to distinguish it from defeat."
>
> *Jean-Paul Sartre*

Speaking in April 2004 to the students and Yogic Flyers at Maharishi University of Management, Dr. Bevan Morris, president of the University, likened the current war in Iraq to being caught in a bear trap. Dr. Morris said:

> Going into Iraq, the U.S. has trapped itself. Either withdrawing results in massive civil war and the U.S. being hated for creating that situation, or it stays, having 100,000 or more younger Americans in harm's way with insurgents and foreign nationals trying to kill them [and the U.S.] hated as an occupying power. The choice is, being hated or being hated.

As Dr. Morris suggests, there is no rational way out of the current crisis. Reason has its limits. The only way to resolve the current crisis in Iraq without increasing the hatred for America, and the only way to *prevent* similar situations in the future, is by increasing support of nature.

Perhaps the most important principle underlying Maharishi's teaching is in the expression *Heyam Duhkham Anagatam*, which means "Avert the danger that has not come," or in the area of defense, "Prevent the birth of an enemy." The Vedic technologies in virtually every area promote strategies of prevention. We will succeed in the war on terrorism only through prevention—only if we can prevent others from becoming our enemies—not from military campaigns aimed at killing our enemies.

"There's a wonderful phrase, 'the fog of war.' What the fog of war means is war is so complex; it's beyond the ability of the human mind to comprehend all the variables. Our judgment, our understanding are not adequate and we kill people unnecessarily.... It isn't that we aren't rational. We are rational, but reason has limits."

Robert S. McNamara
former Secretary of Defense
(from the film The Fog of War *by Errol Morris)*

Maharishi's peaceful, preventive approach includes relatively large groups performing Yogic Flying and engaged in the Yagya performances (40,000 pandits in India, 8,000 Yogic Flyers in the U.S., and 500 pandits in Fairfield, Iowa), as well as a plan to construct Peace Palaces in the world's largest 3,000 cities. Each of these new buildings will be home to a group of 100 to 200 peace-creating experts whose collective practice of the Transcendental Meditation and Yogic Flying programs will help create coherence for their city and contribute to a coherent national consciousness. The administrators at the Peace Palaces will offer a wide range of Maharishi's Vedic peace technologies, including the programs for the prediction and prevention of ill fortune, previously described.

Inspired by Maharishi's desire to create peace in the world, physicist Dr. John Hagelin recently founded the U.S. Peace Government, which will direct the programs in the Peace Palaces. Dr. Hagelin's organization will be a knowledge-based, complementary government, composed of 400 of America's top scientists, health professionals, educators, and other leading experts on the principles of Natural Law. The goal of the U.S. Peace Government is to establish peace-creating groups of Yogic Flyers across America. This includes raising the funds for scholarships and other support for American students desiring to attend Maharishi Vedic University and be part of the U.S. group of 8,000 Yogic Flyers.

The World Is My Family

On an individual level, the experience of the transcendental field creates a bond among people from different cultures because, as even the word "transcendental" suggests, the experience goes beyond, or transcends, individual considerations such as race, religion, and nationality. It makes brothers and sisters of those involved in the Transcendental Meditation technique and Yogic Flying because each meditator knows the other is on a positive and evolutionary path and that real peace and happiness comes from within. On a collective level, it creates an armor of protection for the community.

Maayan Eran from Jerusalem recently learned the Yogic Flying technique in Israel. Writing to Americans who contributed funds for her TM-Sidhi course that included Yogic Flying, she said:

> Today I define myself as a Sidha. I've grown wings, and I can fly. After six years of meditating, from being in the silence, to being the silence, to reach myself and to experience everything that exists in me, this passage is amazing. Every time I am excited all over again to say this word "Sidhi." It is not only words. It is my truth and I experience it every morning when I wake up with a smile on my face with no reason, when I meet people I don't even know and feel like hugging them all, when I look at the sky or at the trees, and they seem to be the most beautiful thing in the world that I simply feel like laughing, just like that.
>
> I want to thank you for giving me the privilege to experience all this, to be part of the music of nature, and to know that it can be much much better. You gave me the power to be happy, and there is nothing more important you could do for Israel. You gave Israel another girl with happiness in her heart that can bring peace....

Payman Salek, a practicing Muslim, received his electrical engineering degree from Tehran Polytechnic and worked in Iran for several years as an electrical engineer. In 1988 Payman learned the Transcendental

Meditation technique in Iran. He became a Yogic Flyer in 1993. Payman told us:

> I was brought up in Iran in a home where religion was not so important. My father actually did not believe in God. As a young boy, I was brought up to believe that the stories about God were just stories to make people feel better, but that God did not exist.
>
> After I learned the Transcendental Meditation technique, from inside I felt the ice melting and the cold feeling that I had about religion and anything spiritual gradually started to change. I started believing in God strongly in the context of my own Muslim religion. My religious practices increased, along with a new respect for everyone's efforts to find their way in the world.
>
> This is a common experience of anyone involved in the TM program. That experience can come either from an individual practicing the TM technique or from being in the vicinity of those practicing the technique.
>
> People may question Maharishi's programs, but they have to know there is no political or educational solution to the problems in Iraq, Iran, Israel, and Palestine. It is impossible to educate everyone using conventional means of education. There are too many poor people to try to educate. However, Maharishi's program wakes the people up and melts their hard feelings, producing the effect that is the goal of a good educational system.

As part of her college program at Maharishi University of Management, Emily Marcus, Jay's daughter, visited India in March 2002. She said:

> When we were in Allahabad we asked the Yagya pandits about their daily activities. They have a very set routine that includes their meditation program and recitations of the Vedic literature to generate their own coherent state. Then they do the Maharishi Yagya performances. The pandits are divided into

groups consisting of from 11 to 1,100 pandits for the Yagya performances that are requested. The number of pandits is determined by the particular Yagya performances.

We went to the very center of India, the area referred to as the *Brahmasthan*. Already, there were 3,000 of Maharishi's Vedic pandits there. We heard them reciting the sounds from several books of the Vedic literature, and it was an amazing experience. The recitation of *Yajur Veda*, for me, was like a wonderful massage. Afterwards I was so serene and blissful.

One day some of the pandits visited us in our hotel because there were no taxis available for us to travel. They had to walk about three hours each way to come see us. When we thanked them for coming, they said *Vasudaiva Kutumbakam* (the world is my family). They told us that we were all part of Maharishi's family and said they would have walked to America if we had wanted to see them. They were so gracious and gentle. It was an amazing experience just to be around them.

Vedic pandits outside New Delhi

Maharishi considers those practicing the Vedic peace technologies to be part of a world family and part of his Global Country of World Peace, created to establish world peace through the Vedic technologies.

Maharishi's Efforts

From the time Maharishi began teaching the Transcendental Meditation program in 1955, he has advocated the program for individual development and world peace. Maharishi explained that the blissful experience of the transcendental field could change a man in a way that was not otherwise possible. And once research showed

> The body of knowledge that Maharishi has rediscovered, Vedic science, is a complete science, which underlies all other science and unites the world of matter with the world of consciousness.

that violence could be reduced in the vicinity of those practicing his peace programs, he began offering his Vedic technologies to governments to protect their homeland and cultivate peace.

In late 2002 and 2003, Dr. John Hagelin and others met with President Bush's deputies for homeland security and congressional leaders to encourage government support for Maharishi's peace programs. Although many in government professed enthusiasm, and seemed to be impressed by the scientific research, as in the past no concrete action has yet been taken by the U.S. government—the typical fate of new paradigms. As a result, Maharishi's programs must be supported privately if they are to succeed. Support is necessary from those who can become Yogic Flyers and those with the resources to support these groups.

Based on Maharishi's efforts to date, there are now millions of TM meditators, 40,000 TM teachers, and many thousands of Yogic Flyers and Vedic peace pandits. While many more are needed, Maharishi has brought us to a position where we now have an opportunity to change the consciousness of the world and prevent acts of mass destruction.

Maharishi's efforts over many years have revived the Vedic wisdom and placed this knowledge on a solid scientific footing. Through the Peace Palaces and the many scientific and educational institutions bearing

Maharishi's name, this knowledge can be preserved in its pure form, and all its practical applications can be investigated.

The body of knowledge that Maharishi has rediscovered, Vedic science, is a complete science, which underlies all other science and unites the world of matter with the world of consciousness. As such, it is the world's principal science and it, alone, can unfold full human potential and create a permanent peace. This revival of the Vedic knowledge in its completeness could only come from a fully developed state of consciousness, a living example of enlightenment. In this age, it is Maharishi whose nervous system is sufficiently refined to allow him to experience the full value of the Vedic knowledge, available at the transcendental level of life.

The Immediate Need for Preventive Action

In today's uncertain times, if we are going to use Maharishi's Vedic technologies on a scale large enough to change world consciousness, there is no time to lose. In the U.S. there are more than 100 nuclear plants that are vulnerable to an attack like that of 9/11. A successful attack would make up to five states uninhabitable for more than 20 years. It would lead to a hugely expensive and massive retaliation, inevitably provoking further terrorist

> None of the conventional institutions can offer any real hope for success in preventing terrorist acts because, as Maharishi explains, suggestions from outside "do not much change the man."

acts. We don't know how many hundreds of thousands of lives would be lost or ruined by such an attack, but it would be catastrophic.

The world is in a precarious position. The increased hatred of religious and other fanatics and the ready availability of weapons of mass destruction present a unique challenge in today's world. None of the conventional institutions can offer any real hope for success in preventing terrorist acts because, as Maharshi explains, suggestions from outside "do not much change the man."

The Vedic knowledge has, for most of modern history, been hidden from public view and not widely available, which accounts for there not being a sufficient number of individuals practicing the Vedic peace technologies to change the collective consciousness of the world. Now, due to Maharishi's efforts, we have a chance to succeed. Like the eternal, unchanging Vedic wisdom, Maharishi's message has been the same from the first days he began the current revival of the Vedic knowledge. Speaking before the 15th session of the World Vegetarian Congress held at Madras, India, on November 30, 1957, Maharishi said:

> How are we going to change the "killing world" of today into a non-killing world of tomorrow? How are we going to change the spirit of killing, the spirit of aggression, the spirit of violence, into the spirit of kindness and love, overflowing love for the whole creation? How are we going to change hardness and cruelty of heart to softness and overflowing love for everybody?

> Through platform speaking? No, it is not possible. Through singing the values of Vegetarianism into the ears of the non-vegetarians? No, because their ears may receive the message but the hardness of their hearts will repel it.

> Suggestive knowledge? Suggestions from outside do not much change the man. Speaking does not go a long way to change a man. All the great religions of the world have been speaking for it from time immemorial. Eternal Vedas have been speaking of it, Holy Bible has been speaking of it, Holy Koran has been speaking of it, yet the killer kills. The killer knows that he is killing and in return he will be killed. The sinner knows that he is committing a sin and that he will be punished for it. Not that he does not know. He knows it. But, with this information, the cruel is not afraid. His cruelty is hardened still.

> The killer declares his action is the role of a savior. He kills in the name of life. He kills in the name of saving life. He kills in the name of maintaining life. He kills and murders ruthlessly in the name of protection and peace. In the name of world peace and protection have been waged the deadliest of wars.

In the name of peace and protection are preparations being made for the murder of man and creation. Shame to the greatness of the human intelligence, which fails to recognize the Judge Supreme!

Our task of the day is to find a cure for this major ill of humanity. The heart of man is so changed. The inner man has to be transformed. A direct experience of the blissful nature of soul, and the inner man is completely transformed. The mind, experiencing the Great Bliss [the transcendental field], feels satisfaction, and this satisfaction of the mind results in right understanding and virtuous action, kindness, love and compassion for all....

The ancient Vedic tradition clearly holds that the Vedic peace technologies can protect any nation from wars and terrorist acts of mass destruction. From research that has been independently reviewed and published in top scientific journals, we know that Maharishi's program results in significant decreases in violence, even when the peace-creating groups are temporary and smaller than what would be necessary to tip the scale toward a complete eradication of the problem. What remains is to establish and maintain permanent groups of experts in the Vedic peace technologies, and demonstrate that a large-scale implementation of Maharishi's program can have the predicted effect of eliminating the threat of mass destruction. If Maharishi's programs are successfully implemented as described in this book, it will be obvious to everyone that what Maharishi has accomplished—a permanent peace and the revival of Vedic wisdom—is the most important achievement of any age, and Maharishi's scientific orientation should cause him to be regarded as both the greatest scientist and the greatest saint of the most profound tradition in mankind's search for knowledge. ■

AFTERWORD*

For 50 years—day and night—Maharishi has been announcing from the rooftops to the whole human race the message of a program for the individual to be in peace, and for the whole world to be in peace.

Maharishi has been making this offer to the world since he began teaching the Transcendental Meditation technique in 1955—this in spite of the fact that we live in an age which has been full of ignorance and violence. The 20th century has been the most violent century in the whole history of the human race: two gigantic wars engulfing the world, hundreds of smaller wars, and a cold war, in which two mighty powers confronted each other with the largest standing armies that ever existed in the world, and 30,000 nuclear weapons on each side.

Into such a world Maharishi came with a message to close the eyes, to transcend and experience the inner peace, the inner bliss, which is Transcendental Consciousness, the Self of every individual. He gave this message in a world where, for example, in America people said to him, "Maharishi, we are practical people, we can't close the eyes, we can't develop our creativity and intelligence and higher consciousness and our good fortune. We are practical people." This was the kind of thinking that Maharishi had to confront right from the very beginning.

I find it just extraordinary that Maharishi continued on and on, traveling alone around the world over and over again, bringing this message to a world so alien to the extreme purity of the valley of the saints in the Himalayas from which he had come, where he had been living in infinite silence and bliss. Yet he didn't seem to mind; he just kept going. He encountered every kind of ignorance, every kind of stress, every kind of impurity, and he is encountering it even today, 50 years later. But he never relented, he never gave up, he never, ever gave up on our human race and the chance that we have in this age to create a world that is permanently peaceful.

And Maharishi did it with such genius, putting his message in all

These remarks have been adapted by Dr. Bevan Morris from his presentation at an international press conference in November, 2004.

the different languages of the world. When he came out of India to America, to Germany, and to other countries that are more accustomed to a scientific language, he brought this great Vedic wisdom, this secret wisdom of the Himalayas, to those countries in *their* language, the language of science. He respected the cultural dignity of each country and did not require that people change either their culture or their religious beliefs. Quite the contrary, they should maintain their own beliefs, while gaining the experience of Transcendental Consciousness—by twice-daily practice of the Transcendental Meditation program, and thereby grow in inner peace, in inner bliss, and become a unit of world peace.

As time unfolded, thousands of people, then hundreds of thousands, and eventually millions were taught to transcend, and 40,000 teachers of Transcendental Meditation were trained in over 100 countries. The mountain of ignorance and stress in the world began to melt, and Maharishi began to probe deeply into the Vedic literature.

The Vedic literature had been thoroughly misunderstood even by such respected Indian scholars as Professor Radhakrishnan. They were completely overshadowed about their own tradition by the views of German scholars, such as Max Mueller, and British scholars. But Maharishi has now restored the reality of what the Vedic teaching is for the whole human race, by diving deeply into the reality of Veda from within his own Self—from the platform of his own Brahman Consciousness, the supreme consciousness where one realizes, *Aham Brahmasmi,* that the individual is nothing but *Brahm,* the totality of consciousness, reverberating as Natural Law, the physiology, and the entire universe.

From that platform of supreme development that he achieved through the teaching of his Master Guru Dev, Maharishi found the Veda to be *Nitya* and *Apauresheya,* an eternal and unmanifest phenomenon. He found it to be Total Knowledge, the totality of all the Laws of Nature that give rise to the physiology, to the solar system, to our galaxy, to billions of galaxies.

This totality of knowledge Maharishi unfolded as a complete science of life, with applications to every field of life—education, health, defense, agriculture, political science, administration, economics, and architecture.

He revealed, for example, that the key to education is the development of higher states of consciousness and development of total brain potential; the key to health—the awakening of the inner intelligence of the body and its relationship to its expression in the physiology; to defense—creating an invincible national consciousness to make the nation impenetrable and to turn any enemy into a friend; to agriculture— attuning all agriculture to be in agreement with Nature's intelligence, so that food is nourishing, health-giving, and uplifting to the whole society; to administration—fulfilling the principle of ideal administration through ideal education—through which all individuals rise to states of higher consciousness, living spontaneously in harmony with the Laws of Nature, so that they neither make mistakes for their own lives nor create a mess in national life that the government has to solve—all problems prevented before they arise.

Maharishi has brought this knowledge out in every field of life, and thanks to him and his Master Guru Dev from whom he obtained this knowledge, we now possess in our age all of the knowledge to make our world into Heaven on Earth.

This heavenly time is described in Vedic Literature as *Raam Raj*, administration from that level of Total Natural Law that administers the universe. It is extraordinary that we now have the chance to live in such an age.

If you go back 50 years to before Maharishi began his teaching, or to any other time in recorded history, the human race has not had the knowledge required to create such a time. Nobody knew how to become enlightened. Nobody knew how to make a nation invincible. Nobody knew how to prevent all diseases, and make society perfectly healthy. Nobody knew how to have a prevention-oriented, ideal administration for a nation. None of that was known. But now Maharishi's gift—his patient gift of Vedic wisdom to the ages—makes all this possible.

In the midst of an age deeply steeped in ignorance, and violence, and miseries of all kinds, Maharishi is creating a different age, a Golden

Age. He has already created it in the sense that he has completely unfold-ed and made totally available to the human race the knowledge that is necessary to make such a Golden Age. So anyone who is awake in the world should come, as Maharishi has said, to take the lighted lamp and fill their own homes with light and their own nation with light. It is that easy. One only has to accept the invitation—take the lighted lamp and fill up the world with light.

When we all bemoan every day the terrible state of the world—the hate-filled conflicts among nations, the horribly self-destructive divisions within nations, the terrible failures of governments and our disgust with the corruption and stupidity of the leaders that we have in the world—when we bemoan all of this, then only a fool would go on in the same direction that we have been going on. We can no longer be fools; we can no longer be stupid people who just carry on as past generations have done with the muddle and mess of politics in every nation and the fail-ures of every government. We should do something different, and fortu-nately we have the chance to do something *completely* different that absolutely works, that is absolutely a proven system of knowledge—that great wisdom of life that can make our world into an entirely different world.

I think that it is so important to thank Maharishi again and again for patiently going on so long, and continuing to give this knowledge to us and to the world, and unfolding more and more details and richness of this knowledge at every step. He is giving every individual human being the chance for liberation, for enlightenment—infinite freedom, life free from suffering—and to our world, the chance to be permanently peace-ful, to be just such a place, as Maharishi has said, where angels would like to reside because it is so perfectly heavenly in our world.

I remember a story that was told long ago about a sage. It is the story of a scorpion that goes into the Ganges and starts to drown, and then the sage saves the scorpion and the scorpion stings the sage. Then the scorpion goes back into the water and starts to drown again. Again, the sage goes and rescues the scorpion, and the scorpion stings. After a few times like this, the people looking on are saying, "What kind of man is this?" And they ask him, "Why do you keep doing this, when the scorpion keeps stinging?" And the sage says, "It is the scorpion's nature to sting, but it is my nature to save."

I think that this is just the story of Maharishi in the midst of this age, which in India is called *Kali Yuga*, a time of darkness, violence, stress, and strain that has been going on these last 5,000 years or so. We see the violence in the world—we see people like tigers pouncing—and there is no point in our trying to persuade them not to be tigers, because that is their nature. But what Maharishi offers to those in this world who have a peaceful heart, who have a peaceful wish for the human race, is that they just take up this knowledge, and put it in their schools and colleges and universities for the children to rise in peace. The result will be that all of this violent nature that exists in the world will simply disappear. It will just quietly evaporate before our eyes. This is the chance that is before us today—to change the destiny of our human race.

A peaceful age, a Golden Age, is coming: it is seen on the horizon by the wise. Maharishi sees it coming and all of the wise of the world know that a better time, a golden time, is coming, in spite of all that we see about us yet in the world today. And this time is coming just because of the supreme genius of His Holiness Maharishi Mahesh Yogi and his perfect representation of the total knowledge that he received at the feet of his Master Guru Dev, His Divinity Brahmananda Saraswati, the Jagad Guru Shankaracharya of Jyotir Math in the Himalayas, the supreme of the supreme—whose gift of total knowledge is perfectly represented in our world by this giant sage, this great sage, this compassionate sage of the Vedic tradition of Masters, His Holiness Maharishi Mahesh Yogi.

—*Dr. Bevan Morris*
Dr. Bevan Morris is president and chairman of the Board of Trustees of Maharishi University of Management, in Fairfield, Iowa, and Minister of Enlightenment of the Global Country of World Peace. For 36 years he has been one of the principal teachers of Maharishi's Vedic peace technologies, including the Yogic Flying program. He is the foremost expert on Maharishi's Vedic approach to education and has traveled widely throughout the world to implement Maharishi's teachings.

APPENDIX A

Flying through the Ages

The history of flying is both ancient and modern. In the oldest records of human experience, in the Vedic literature, and in reports about saintly persons in the West, we find detailed descriptions of both the phenomenon and the technique of flying.

Reports of Flying through the Ages

"Levitation, the name given to the raising of the human body from the ground by no apparent physical force, is recorded in some form or other in over two hundred saints and holy persons (as well as in many others)...."

from *Butler's Lives of the Saints*

"When the Yogi though remaining in Padmasana [sitting position] can rise in the air and leave the ground, then know that he has gained Vayu-siddhi (success over air), which destroys the darkness of the world.... It destroys decay and death."

from *The Siva Samhita,* trans. Raj Bahadur Srisa Chandra Vasu
(India: Sat Guru Publications, 1984)

"He [St. Joseph of Copertino] at once flew about a dozen paces over the heads of those present to the foot of the statue. Then after paying homage there...uttering his customary shrill cry he flew back again and straightway returned to his cell, leaving the Admiral, his wife, and the large retinue which attended them speechless with astonishment."

translated in *The Physical Phenomena of Mysticism,*
Herbert Thurston, S. J., from Acta Sanctorum, Sep. Vol. V,
Angelo Pastrovicchi (London: Burns & Oates, 1952)

"During the seventeen years he [St. Joseph of Copertino] remained at Grottella over seventy occasions are recorded of his levitation."

from *Butler's Lives of the Saints, Complete Edition*,
edited, revised and supplemented by Herbert Thurston, S.J.,
and Donald Attwater (New York: P.J. Kennedy & Sons, 1962)

"Rapture is generally irresistible… it sweeps upon you so swift and strong that you see and feel yourself being caught up in this cloud and borne aloft as on the wings of a mighty eagle…. Even at times my whole body has been lifted from the ground."

translated from the words of St. Teresa of Avila,
in *St. Teresa of Avila*, Stephen Clissold (London: Sheldon Press, 1982)

"He was sitting on a mat, like all the others, in the usual Buddha position. Suddenly, he sprang off his seat into the air, easily two-and-a-half to three metres high, at least well above my head—I am 1.91 metres tall—and then relatively slowly, certainly much more slowly than a man landing from a jump, he landed again in his Buddha position. I was very much surprised, for it was absolutely clear that this was no usual jump, but a true but quick levitation."

translated from *Magier, Machte and Mysterien*, Wilhelm Moufang
(Heidelberg: Keysersche Verlagsbuchhandlung, 1954)

"I found myself lifted up completely by the very soles of my feet, just as the magnet draws up a fragment of iron, but with a gentleness that was marvellous and most delightful…. I knew that I was raised some distance above the earth, my whole body being suspended for a considerable space of time. Down to last Christmas eve (1618) this happened to me on five different occasions."

translated from the words of Sour Maria Villani, in
***The Physical Phenomena of Mysticism*, Herbert Thurston, S.J., from**
***Vita della V. Serva di Dio Sour Maria Villani*, D.M. Marchese**
(London: Burns & Oates, 1952)

"When one sits in meditation, the fleshly body becomes quite shining like silk or jade. It seems difficult to remain sitting; one feels as if drawn upwards.... In time, one can experience it in such a way that one really floats upward."

from *The Secret of the Golden Flower, A Chinese Book of Life,*
trans. Richard Wilhelm (London:
Kegan Paul, Trench, Trubner & Co., Ltd., 1962)

"St. Richard, then chancellor to St. Edmund, Archbishop of Canterbury, one day softly opening the chapel door, to see why the archbishop did not come to dinner, saw him raised high in the air, with his knees bent and his arms stretched out...."

from *The Origins of Culture,* Sir Edward Burnett
Tylor (New York: Harper & Row, 1958)

"One effect of Thomas's amazing concentration in prayer was that several times, as he prayed, his body was seen lifted off the ground, as if it followed the movement of his mind...."

from 'The Life of St. Thomas Aquinas', Bernard Gui
in *The Life of Saint Thomas Aquinas: Biographical Documents,*
trans. and ed. Kenelm Foster, O.P. (Baltimore: Helicon Press, 1959)

Yogic Flying

Despite the many instances of levitation over the centuries, flying was not a part of modern life until the late summer of 1986. Then, for the first time in modern history, hundreds of people demonstrated the first stage of Yogic Flying in front of thousands of witnesses while millions more watched the performances on television in their own homes. In the first stage of Yogic Flying the body lifts off the ground in a series of hops, not based on a gymnastic effort, but on a mental performance. In the second stage, the body levitates. In the third stage, "passage through the air" or flying is predicted. To date Maharishi's Yogic Flyers have experienced the first stage of Yogic Flying.

Experiences of Yogic Flyers

"When my body lifts up into the air, I feel a great strengthening of the physiology, and my mind is filled with a feeling of joy, vitality, and brilliance."

N.G., Britain

"During the practice of Yogic Flying, I feel very light, strong, and invincible. The more silence I experience inwardly, the higher is the flying and the greater the bliss."

A.R., Czechoslovakia

"The experience during Yogic Flying is one of complete silence and peace followed by very powerful thrills of bliss that literally propel the body into the air."

P.B., Switzerland

"The act of Yogic Flying is totally automatic and effortless. When the mind is completely calm, just the smallest intention to fly is enough to lift my body up and propel it forward on a wave of energy and happiness."

J.K., U.S.

"The subjective experience of Yogic Flying is a feeling of the body being composed of bliss, or pure joy, rather than some heavy material substance."

T.S., Dominica

"During the [Yogic Flying] demonstration, there was a feeling of great expansiveness, as though consciousness had filled the hall. The whole time it seemed as though I was moving about very freely and effortlessly in that feeling. This expansiveness completely dominated the experience. I was not so much aware of the body except to know that it was very light and moving about in a very blissful, energetic, and silent manner."

B.W., Canada

"When my body lifts up in the air, I feel an enormous inner peace and integration of heart, mind, body, and surroundings. There is a feeling of togetherness with everyone and everything."

G.K.P., Norway

"The more people around me practicing the TM-Sidhi 'yogic flying' technique, the more I can enjoy it."

T.P., Finland

APPENDIX B

More information on the Vedic peace technologies may be obtained from the following:

United States Peace Government
1000 North Fourth Street
Fairfield, Iowa 52557
(641) 472-1200
(641) 472-1165 Fax

For information on enrolling in Maharishi Vedic Universities or participating in Yogic Flying groups, contact:

Maharishi University of Management
Office of Admissions
Fairfield, Iowa 52557
(800) 369-6480
admissions@mum.edu

For Internet information:

www.victorybeforewar.com

www.permanentpeace.org

www.tm.org

www.mum.edu

www.maharishivediccity.com

NOTES

Chapter One

1. A book on Yogic Flying and the experience of flying throughout the ages will soon be published. See, Pearson, C., *The Complete Book of Yogic Flying*, Maharishi University of Management Press, Fairfield, Iowa, 2005, in press.

2. Borland, C., and Landrith, III, G., "Improved Quality of City Life Through the Transcendental Meditation Program: Decreased Crime Rate," *Scientific Research on the Transcendental Meditation and TM-Sidhi Program: Collected Papers* (hereafter this reference is to *Collected Papers*), Vol. 1, 1976, p. 639.

3. Davies, J.L., and Alexander, C.N., "The Maharishi Technology of the Unified Field and Improved Quality of Life in the United States: A Study of the First World Peace Assembly, Amherst, Massachusetts, 1979," *Collected Papers*, Vol. 4, 1989, p. 2549.

4. Hagelin, J.S., Rainforth, M.V., Orme-Johnson, D.W., Cavanaugh, K.L., Alexander, C.N., Shatkin, S.F., Davies, J.L., Hughes, A.O., and Ross, E., "Effects of group practice of the Transcendental Meditation program on preventing violent crime in Washington, D.C.: Results of the National Demonstration Project, June–July, 1993," *Social Indicators Research*, 47(2): 153–201 (1999).

Chapter Two

1. Terrorism in the United States 1999, U.S. Dept. of Justice, Federal Bureau of Investigation, 1999, p. 16.

2. *The 9/11 Report*, St. Martin's Paperbacks, New York, p. 536.

3. Maharishi Mahesh Yogi, *The Science of Being and Art of Living*, New American Library Signet Book, New York, 1963, pp. 86–87.

Chapter Three

1. Nader, T., *Human Physiology: Expressions of Veda and the Vedic Literature,* Maharishi Vedic University Press, Vlodrop, Holland, 1995, pp. 144–162.

2. Maharishi Mahesh Yogi, *Ideal India,* Maharishi Vedic University Press, Vlodrop, Holland, 2001, pp. 69–70.

Chapter Four

1. Wallace, R.K., Benson, H., and Wilson, A.F., "A Wakeful Hypometabolic Physiologic State," *American Journal of Physiology,* Vol. 221, 1971, pp. 795–799.

2. Wallace, R.K., "Physiological Effects of Transcendental Meditation," *Science,* Vol. 167, 1970, pp. 751–754.

3. Wallace, R.K., and Benson, H., "The Physiology of Meditation," *Scientific American,* Vol. 226 (2), 1972, pp. 84–90.

4. Jevning, R., Wilson, A.F., and Davidson, J.M., "Adrenocortical Activity During Meditation," *Hormones and Behavior,* Vol. 10, No. 1, 1978, pp. 54–60; Werner, O.R., Wallace, R.K., Charles, B., Janssen, G., Stryker, T., & Chalmers, R. A., "Long-term Endocrinologic Changes in Subjects Practicing the Transcendental Meditation and TM-Sidhi program," *Psychosomatic Medicine,* Vol. 48, 1986, pp. 59–66.

5. Bujatti, M. and Riederer, P., "Serotonin, Noradrenaline, Dopamine Metabolites in Transcendental Meditation," *Journal of Neural Transmission,* Vol. 39, 1976, p. 257; Walton, K.G., Lerom, M., Salerno, J., and Wallace, R.K., "Practice of the Transcendental Meditation and TM-Sidhi Program May Affect the Circadian Rhythm of Urinary 5 - Hydroxyindole Excretion," *Society for Neuroscience Abstracts*, Vol. 7, 1981, p. 48.

6. Banquet, J., "Spectral Analysis of the EEG in Meditation," *Electroencephalography and Clinical Neurophysiology*, Vol. 35, 1973, pp. 143–151; Levine, P.H., Herbert, J.R., Haynes, C.T., and Strobel, U., "EEG Coherence During the Transcendental Meditation Technique," *Collected Papers*, Vol. 1, 1976, p. 187.

7. Banquet, J., "Spectral Analysis of the EEG in Meditation," *Electroencephalography and Clinical Neurophysiology*, Vol. 35, 1973, pp. 143–151.

8. Levine, P.H., Herbert, J.R., Haynes, C.T., and Strobel, U., "EEG Coherence During the Transcendental Meditation Technique," *Collected Papers*, Vol. 1, 1976, p. 187.

9. Travis, F., "Autonomic and EEG Patterns Distinguish Transcending from Other Experiences during Transcendental Meditation Practice," *International Journal of Psychophysiology*, Vol. 42(1), 2001, pp. 1-9; Travis, F., J. J. Tecce, et al., "Cortical Plasticity, Contingent Negative Variation, and Transcendent Experiences during Practice of the Transcendental Meditation Technique," *Biological Psychology*, Vol. 55(1), 2000, pp. 41-55; Travis, F. and R. K. Wallace, "Autonomic and EEG Patterns during Eyes-closed Rest and Transcendental Meditation (TM) Practice; the Basis for a Neural Model of TM practice," *Consciousness and Cognition*, Vol. 8(3), 1999, pp. 302-18; Travis, F. T., "Eyes Open and TM EEG Patterns after One and After Eight Years of TM Practice," *Psychophysiology*, Vol. 28(3a), 1991, p. S58; Travis, F. T., J. Tecce, et al., "Patterns of EEG Coherence, Power, and Contingent Negative Variation Characterize the Integration of Transcendental and Waking States," *Biological Psychology*, Vol. 61, 2002, pp. 293–319.

10. Travis, F.T., and Orme-Johnson, D.W., "EEG Coherence and Power during Yogic Flying," *International Journal of Neuroscience,* Vol. 54, 1990, p. 1; Orme-Johnson, D.W., Clements, G., Haynes, C.T., Bodaori, K., "Higher States of Consciousness: EEG Coherence, Creativity, and Experience of the Sidhis," *Collected Papers,* Vol. 1, 1976, p. 707.

11. Physicist Lawrence Domash was the first to describe the parallel functioning of coherent states of matter and coherent states of consciousness. Many of the examples in this chapter are derived from lectures by Dr. Domash for courses he developed in physics and consciousness presented at Maharishi University of Management in Fairfield, Iowa.

Chapter Five

1. Borland, C., and Landrith, III, G., "Improved Quality of City Life through the Transcendental Meditation Program: Decreased Crime Rate," *Collected Papers,* Vol. 1, 1976, p. 639.

2. Dillbeck, M.C., Landrith, III, G.S., Polanzi, C., and Baker, S.R., "The Transcendental Meditation Program and Crime Rate Change: A Causal Analysis," *Collected Papers,* Vol. 4, 1989, pp. 2515–2520.

3. Dillbeck, M.C., Foss, A.P.O., and Zimmermann, W.J., "Maharishi's Global Ideal Society Campaign: Improved Quality of Life in Rhode Island through the Transcendental Meditation and TM-Sidhi Program," *Collected Papers,* Vol. 4, 1989, p. 2521.

4. Davies, J.L., and Alexander, C.N., "The Maharishi Technology of the Unified Field and Improved Quality of Life in the United States: A Study of the First World Peace Assembly, Amherst, Massachusetts, 1979," *Collected Papers,* Vol. 4, 1989, p. 2549.

5. Burgmans, W.H.P.M., Van der Burgt, A.T., and Langenkamp, F.P.Th., "Sociological Effects of the Group Dynamics of Consciousness: Decrease of Crime and Traffic Accidents in Holland," *Collected Papers,* Vol. 4, 1989, p. 2566.

6. Hagelin, J.S., Rainforth, M.V., Orme-Johnson, D.W., Cavanaugh, K.L., Alexander, C.N., Shatkin, S.F., Davies, J.L., Hughes, A.O., and Ross, E., "Effects of group practice of the Transcendental Meditation program on preventing violent crime in Washington, D.C.: Results of the National Demonstration Project, June-July, 1993," *Social Indicators Research,* 47(2): 153-201 (1999).

7. See, for example, Dillbeck, M.C., Banus, C.B., Polanzi, C., and Landrith III, G.S., "Test of a Field Model of Consciousness and Social Change: The Transcendental Meditation and TM-Sidhi Program and Decreased Urban Crime," *The Journal of Mind and Behavior,* Vol. 9, No. 4, 1988, pp. 457–486; Dillbeck, M.C., Landrith III, G., and Orme-Johnson, D.W., "The Transcendental Meditation Program and Crime Rate Change in a Sample of Forty-eight Cities," *Journal of Crime and Justice,* Vol. 4, 1981, pp. 25–45; Orme-Johnson, D.W., Alexander, C.N., Davies, J.L., Chandler, H.M., and Larimore, W.E., "International Peace Project in the Middle East: The Effect of the Maharishi Technology of the Unified Field," *Journal of Conflict Resolution,* Vol. 32, No. 4, 1988, pp. 776–812.

Chapter Seven

1. Radwan, A., "Portrait of the Terrorist as a Young Man," *Time.com,* November 13, 2001.

2. Krantz, C., "Afghanistan war reports evoke strong feelings in Iowans," *Des Moines Register,* November 1, 2001.

3. Kotulak, R., "How Brain's Chemistry Unleashes Violence," *Chicago Tribune,* December 13, 1993.

4. Ibid.

5. Ibid.

6. Coccaro, E., "Central Serotonin and Impulsive Aggression," *British Journal of Psychiatry,* Vol. 155, Supplement 8, 1989, pp. 52–62.

7. Kotulak, "How Brain's Chemistry" (see note 3, this Chapter).

8. Bujatti, M., and Riederer, P., "Serotonin, Noradrenaline, Dopamine Metabolites in Transcendental Meditation," *Journal of Neural Transmission,* Vol. 39, 1976, p. 257.

9. Walton, K.G., Lerom, M., Salerno, J., and Wallace, R.K., "Practice of the TM and TM-Sidhi Program May Affect the Circadian Rhythm of Five-Hydroxyindole Excretion," *Society for Neuroscience Abstracts,* Vol. 7, 1981, p. 48.

10. Jevning, R., Wilson, A.F., and Davidson, J.M., "Adrenocortical Activity during Meditation," *Hormones and Behavior,* Vol. 10, No. 1, 1978; pp. 54-60; Jevning, R., Wallace, R.K., and Beiderbach, M., "The Physiology of Meditation: A Review: A Wakeful Hypometabolic Integrated Response," *Neuroscience and Bio-Behavioral Review,* Vol. 16, 1992, pp. 415–424.

11. Walton, K.G., and Levitsky, D.K., "Effects of the Transcendental Meditation Program on Neuroendocrine Abnormalities Associated with Aggression and Crime," in *Transcendental Meditation in Criminal Rehabilitation and Crime Prevention,* Haworth Press, 2003, pp. 67–87; MacLean, C.R.K., Walton, K.G., Wenneberg, S.R., Levitsky, D.K., Mandarino, J.B., Wazari, R., Hillis, S.L., and Schneider, R.H., "Effects of the Transcendental Meditation program on Adaptive Mechanisms: Changes in Hormone Levels and Responses to Stress after 4 Months of Practice," *Psychoneuroendocrinology,* Vol. 22, 1997, pp. 227–295.

12. Knoblich, G., and King, R., "Biological Correlates of Criminal Behavior," in *Facts, Frameworks and Forecasts,* ed. McCord, Vol. 3, Transaction Publishers, New Brunswick, NJ, 1992, pp. 4–5.

13. Venables, P.H., "Psychophysiology and Crime: Theory and Data," in *Biological Contributions to Crime Cessation,* ed., Moffitt and Mednick, Martinus Nighoff, Boston, 1988, p. 78.

14. Goleman, D.J., and Schwartz, G.E., "Meditation as an intervention in stress reactivity," *Journal of Consulting and Clinical Psychology,* Vol. 44(3), 1976, pp. 456–466.

15. Brennan, P., Mednick, S., and Volavka, J., "Biomedical Factors in Crime," in *Crime,* ed. Wilson and Peterselia, Institute for Contemporary Studies, San Francisco, 1995, p. 86.

Chapter Eight

1. *Terrorism in the United States* 1999, U.S. Dept. of Justice, Federal Bureau of Investigation, 1999, p. 16.

2. Beck, A.J., "Recidivism of Prisoners Released in 1983," U.S. Dept. of Justice, April, 1989.

3. Evans, B., "Health Check," *A.C.M.I. First Step Newsletter,* Vol. 22, Georgia Dept. of Corrections, 1994, p. 3.

4. Ellis, G.A., *Inside Folsom Prison,* ETC Publications, Palm Springs, CA, 1979, p. 170.

5. Abrams, A.I., and Siegel, L.M., "TheTranscendental Meditation Program and Rehabilitation at Folsom State Prison: A Cross-Validation Study," *Collected Papers,* Vol. 3, 1989, pp. 2093–2103; see also Abrams, A.I., and Siegel, L.M., "Transcendental Meditation and Rehabilitation at Folsom Prison: Response to a Critique," *Criminal Justice and Behavior,* Vol. 6, No. 1, 1974, pp. 13–21; and see Abrams, A.I., "A Follow-up Study of the Effects of the Transcendental Meditation Program on Inmates at Folsom Prison," *Collected Papers,* Vol. 3, 1989, pp. 2108–2112.

6. Ramirez, J., "The Transcendental Meditation Program as a Possible Treatment Modality for Drug Offenders: Evaluation of a Pilot Project at Milan Federal Correctional Institute," *Collected Papers,* Vol. 2, 1989, pp. 1118–1134.

7. Ferguson, R., "The Transcendental Meditation Program at the Massachusetts Correctional Institution Walpole: An Evaluation Report," *Collected Papers,* Vol. 2, 1989, pp. 1146–1155.

8. Ballou, D., "The Transcendental Meditation Program at Stillwater Prison," *Collected Papers,* Vol. 1, 1976, pp. 569–576.

9. Gore, S., Abrams, A., and Ellis, G., "The Effect of Statewide Implementation of the Maharishi Technology of the Unified Field in the Vermont Department of Corrections," *Collected Papers,* Vol. 3, 1989, pp. 2453–2464.

10. Bleick, C.R., and Abrams, A.I., "The Transcendental Meditation Program and Criminal Recidivism in California," *Journal of Criminal Justice,* Vol. 15, 1987, pp. 212–215.

11. Alexander, C.N., Grant, J., and Stadte, C. Von., "The Effects of the Transcendental Meditation Technique on Recidivism: A Retrospective Archival Analysis," doctoral thesis of first author, Dept. of Psychology and Social Relations, Harvard University, Cambridge, 1982.

12. Anklesaria, F.H., and King, Michael S., "The Enlightened Sentencing Project," *Journal of Offender Rehabilitation* (in press).

Chapter Nine

1. Nader, T., *Human Physiology: Expression of the Veda and the Vedic Literature,* Maharishi Vedic University Press, Vlodrop, Holland, 1995, pp. 294–305.

2. Ibid., pp. 303–305.

Chapter Ten

1. Maharishi Mahesh Yogi, *Bhagavad-Gita, a New Translation and Commentary, Chapters 1–6,* Age of Enlightenment Press, Fairfield, Iowa, 1967.

2. Ibid., p. 351.

Chapter Eleven

1. Stern, J., *The Ultimate Terrorists,* Harvard University Press, Cambridge, Mass., 1999, pp. 80–81.

2. Goode, E., "Attackers Believed To Be Sane," *The New York Times,* September 12, 2001.

3. Ibid.

4. Marcus, J.B., *Success from Within,* Maharishi University of Management Press, Fairfield, IA, 1990, p. 160.

5. Barrash J., Tramel, D., Anderson, S.W., "Acquired personality disturbances associated with bilateral damage to the ventro-medial prefrontal region," *Dev. Neuropsychology,* Vol. 18 (3), 2000, pp. 355–81.

6. Moll, J., Eslinger, P.J., Oliveira-Souza, R.D., "Frontopolar and Anterior Temporal Cortex Activation in a Moral Judgment Task: Preliminary Functional MRI Results in Normal Subjects," *Arq. Europsiquiatr,* Vol. 59 (3-B), September, 2001, pp. 657–664 ; Moll, J., Oliveira-Souza, R.D., Eslinger, P.J., Bramati, I.E., Mourao-Miranda, J., Andreiuolo, P.A., Pessoa, L., "The Neural Correlates of Moral Sensitivity: a Functional Magnetic Resonance Imaging Investigation of Basic and Moral Emotions," *Journal of Neuroscience,* Vol. 22 (7), April 2001, pp. 2730-2736; and Moll, J., Oliveira-Souza, R.D., Bramati, I.E., Grafman, J., "Functional Networks in Emotional Moral and Nonmoral Social Judgments," *Neuroimage,* Vol. 16, July 2002, pp. 696–703.

7. Lyubimov, N.N., "Changes in Electroencephalogram and Evoked Potentials during Application of the Specific Form of Physiological Training (Meditation)," *Human Physiology,* Vol. 25, No.2, 1998, pp. 171–180.

8. Nidich, S.I., Nidich, R., Abrams, A., Orme-Johnson, D.W., and Wallace, R.K., "Frontal Lobe Functioning: EGG Coherence as a Predictor of Highly Pro-Social Behavior with Subjects Practicing the Transcendental Meditation and TM-Sidhi Program," *Collected Papers,* Vol. 4, 1982, pp. 2277–2282.

9. Nidich, S.I., and Nidich, R., "The Transcendental Meditation and TM-Sidhi Program and Moral Development," *Collected Papers,* Vol. 3, 1983, pp. 2034–2037.

10. Nidich, R., and Nidich, S.I., "An Empirical Study of the Moral Atmosphere at Maharishi International University/University High School," *Collected Papers, V*ol. 4, 1983, pp. 2407–2413.

11. Nidich, S.I., "A Study of the Relationship of the Transcendental Meditation Program to Kohlberg's Stages of Moral Reasoning," *Collected Papers,* 1975, Vol. 1, pp. 585–593.

12. Maharishi Mahesh Yogi, *Maharishi Mahesh Yogi on the Bhagavad Gita, A New Translation and Commentary,* Penguin Press, Middlesex, England, 1967, pp. 155–161.

Chapter 12

1. Tompkins and Bird, *The Secret Life of Plants,* note 1, Chapter 1, pp. 145–148.

2. Retallack, Dorothy, *The Sound of Music and Plants,* DeVoiss & Co., Santa Monica, Ca., 1973.

3. Orme-Johnson, D.W., "Medical Core Utilization and the Transcendental Meditation Program," *Psychosomatic Medicine,* Vol. 49 (1987) 493–507; Herron, R.E., Schneider, R.H., Mandarino , J.V., Alexander, C.N. and Walton, K.G., "Cost-Effective Hypertension Management: Comparison of Drug Therapies with an Alternative Program," *The American Journal of Managed Care,* Vol. 2, No. 4, pp. 427-437; Herron, R.E., and Hillis, S.L., 1986, "The Impact of the Transcendental Meditation Program on Government Payments to Physicians in Quebec: An Update," The American Journal of Health Promotion, Vol. 14(5), 2000, pp. 284–291.

4. Schneider, R.H., Staggers, F., Alexander, C., Sheppard, W., Rainforth, M., Kondwani, K., Smith, S. and King, C.G., "A randomized controlled trial of stress reduction for hypertension in older African Americans," *Hypertension,* Vol. 26, 1995, pp. 820–827; Schneider, R. H., Alexander., C.N., Wallace, R. K., "In Search of an Optimal Behavioral Treatment for Hypertension: A Review and Focus on Transcendental Meditation," in *Personality, Elevated Blood Pressure, and Essential Hypertension,* H. Johnson, W.D. Gentry, and S. Julius (eds., Hemisphere Publishing, Washington, D.C., pp. 291–316; Castillo-Richmond, A., Schneider, R.S., Alexander, C., Cook, R., Meyers, H., Haney, C. and Rainforth, M., "Effects of the Transcendental Meditation Program on carotid atherosclerosis (abstract)," *Ethnicity and Disease,* Vol. 8(2) 1998, p. 287; Zamarra, J.W., Schneider, R.H., Besseghini, I., Robinson, D.K. and Salerno, J.W., "Usefulness of the Transcendental Meditation Program in the Treatment of Patients with Coronary Artery Disease," *American Journal of Cardiology,* Vol. 78, 1996, pp. 77–80; Schneider, R., Nidich, S., Salerno, J., Sharma, H., Robinson, C., Nidich, R. and Alexander, C.M., "Lower Lipid Peroxide Levels in Practitioners of the Transcendental Meditation Program," *Psychosomatic Medicine,* Vol. 60, 1998, pp. 38–41;

Barnes, V.A., Trieber, F.A., Davis, H., and Strong, W.B., "Impact of Transcendental Meditation on Cardiovascular Function at Rest and During Acute Stress in Adolescents with High Normal Blood Pressure," *Journal of Psychosomatic Research,* Vol. 51, 2001, pp. 597–605; Schneider, R., Alexander, C., Staggers, F., Orme-Johnson, D., Rainforth, M., Salerno, J., Sheppard, W., Castillo-Richmond, A., Barnes, V. and Nidich, S., "A Randomized Controlled Trial of Stress Reduction in the Treatment of Hypertension in African Americans Over One Year," *American Journal of Hypertension* (in press).

5. Marcus, J.B., *The Crime Vaccine,* Claitor's Books, Baton Rouge, LA, 1996, pp. 124–133.

6. Eppley, K., Abrams, A., and Shear, J.,"The Effects of Meditation and Relaxation Techniques on Trait Anxiety, a Meta-Analysis," presented at the Convention of the American Psychological Association (Toronto, Canada), August 1984; Dillbeck, M.C. "The Effect of the Transcendental Meditation Technique on Anxiety Level," *Journal of Clinical Psychology,* Vol. 33, 1977, pp. 79-881; 1076–1078; Dillbeck , M. C., and Orme-Johnson, D. W., "Physiological Differences between Transcendental Meditation and Rest," *American Psychologist,* Vol. 42, 1987, pp. 879–881; and Orme-Johnson, D. and Walton, K.G., "All Approaches to Preventing or Reversing Effects of Stress are Not the Same," *American Journal of Health Promotion,* Vol. 12 (5), 1998, pp. 297–299.

7. Nader, T., Smith, D., Dillbeck, M., Schanbacher, V., Dillbeck, S., Gallois, P., Beall-Rougerie, S., Schneider, R., Nidich, S., Kaplan, G. and Belok, S., "A Double Blind Randomized Controlled Trial of Maharishi Vedic Vibration Technology in Subjects With Arthritis," *Frontiers in Bioscience,* Vol. 6, 2001, pp. 7–17.

FURTHER ACKNOWLEDGMENTS

We especially thank Dr. Bevan Morris for his support for this book, for his suggestions on the book's organization and contents, and for his insights into Maharishi's knowledge. We thank Dr. John Hagelin for his suggestions on the book and for his lead in implementing Maharishi's programs and organizing research to demonstrate their effectiveness. We thank Bonnie Barnett for her editing and extensive assistance in helping us to accurately describe Maharishi's programs. We are also grateful to Martha Bright and Burton Milward, Jr., for their editing assistance. Our gratitude to Liz Howard and Carolyn Boyce for the book's layout and design and to Shana Cordon for her illustrations. We thank our agent, Ben Camardi, at the Harold Matson Agency, for his support, friendship, and advice over the years. We thank Craig Pearson for photographs of Yogic Flyers and Tom Egenes for photographs of Vedic pandits. We thank Farrokh Anklesaria for certain interviews with judges, inmates, and correctional officers involved in the use of the Transcendental Meditation program in correctional institutions. We thank Becky Ewing for typing the manuscript and her dedicated and faithful support over many years. Finally, we thank our wives and children for their devoted support and suggestions. ∎

ABOUT THE AUTHORS

Dr. Robert Keith Wallace is a prominent neurophysiologist who conducted ground-breaking research in the 1970s at UCLA and Harvard, documenting the physiological changes occurring during the practice of the Transcendental Meditation technique. Dr. Wallace's research, published in *Science, Scientific American,* and the *American Journal of Physiology*, has led to thousands of research studies and articles on meditation, and to the widespread acceptance of meditation in the Western world. Dr. Wallace is the author of several books on the neurophysiology of higher states of consciousness. In this book he turns his attention to Maharishi's advanced programs and demonstrates how they can peacefully prevent terrorism. Dr. Wallace received his undergraduate degree in physics and his doctorate in physiology from UCLA. He was the Founding President and is currently a Trustee and Chairman of the Department of Physiology and Health at Maharishi University of Management in Fairfield, Iowa.

Jay Marcus is an attorney and the author of three prior books on the use of the Transcendental Meditation program for stress reduction. From 1990 to 1993 Mr. Marcus was chairman of the permanent ethics committee for business lawyers in the state of Iowa. Mr. Marcus is a Phi Beta Kappa graduate of Rutgers University. He received his law degree from the University of Virginia Law School and practiced corporate and securities law in New York City and Los Angeles before moving to Fairfield, Iowa in 1982, where he now practices law. Mr. Marcus learned the Transcendental Meditation technique in 1972 and became a Yogic Flyer in 1977. ■